MASTERING BUSINESS AND FINANCE STRATEGIES FOR SUCCESS

Across Entrepreneurship, Investment, and Economic Management

By: Mujahid Bakht

Hardcover: ISBN 979-8-89302-030-4

Paperback: ISBN 979-8-89302-031-1

EBook: ISBN 979-8-89302-032-8

Published By:

Atlas Amazon, LLC.

244 Fifth Avenue, #D210

New York, NY 10001 USA

Second Edition - 2025

DISCLAIMER

This book is for informational purposes only, based on personal experiences, research, and insights. While every effort has been made to ensure accuracy, the author is not responsible for any decisions, risks, or outcomes resulting from the use of this information.

1st Edition Published in 2023.

TABLE OF CONTENTS

Foreword

This book offers a straightforward introduction to the essentials of business and finance, catering to newcomers and those looking to refresh their knowledge. It covers a wide range of topics, including the basics of setting up and running various types of businesses, from sole proprietorships to corporations, and delves into the different financing options available, such as equity, debt, and venture capital.

We also explore financial planning and analysis, which is crucial for maintaining the health of a business. You'll learn how to create budgets, forecast economic trends, and analyze statements like balance sheets, income statements, and cash flow statements to make well-informed decisions.

Investment management is another key area discussed in this book. It includes strategies for managing assets, handling risks, and diversifying investment portfolios. You'll understand the different types of investments available, including stocks, bonds, and mutual funds, and learn how to evaluate their risks and potential returns.

Managing risks is vital for any business or financial institution. This book outlines the types of risks you might face, such as credit risk, market risk, and operational risk, and suggests strategies to manage them effectively.

Understanding corporate finance is essential to managing daily finances and risks. This section of the book covers important topics like capital budgeting, how businesses structure their capital, and policies on dividends. It explains various sources of capital—such as debt, equity, and retained earnings—and how companies can use these funds to grow and operate efficiently.

Throughout the book, we use practical examples and case studies to illustrate these concepts, making the information engaging and applicable to real-world situations. These examples help bridge the gap between theoretical knowledge and practical application, providing you with the tools you need to make savvy financial decisions.

This book is designed to be an essential resource for anyone looking to delve into the field of business and finance. Whether you're starting a career, running a business, or simply looking to improve your financial knowledge, this book will equip you with the necessary skills and understanding to navigate the complexities of the financial world with confidence.

LIFE HISTORY Mr. Bakht is a mature, experienced, extremely enthusiastic, energetic, administrator, and thirty-six years have proven experience as a businessman in international marketing and public relations. Mr. Bakht is an International Real Estate Specialist, and Professional Business and Projects Consultant. He was born in Pakistan, Educated in Pakistan and USA. Presently American Citizen belongs to a business-oriented family. Thirty-Six years Resident of New York, USA.

BUSINESS HISTORY: Mr. Bakht is a Founder & President of Atlas Amazon, LLC., Mr. Bakht is a business developer and multilingual business specialist in the Caribbean, South East Asia, and the Middle East emerging markets Mr. Bakht has served, met, and host many heads of the States. Also, maintain a close relationship with investors of high net worth in the USA.

CAREER: Mr. Bakht has been engaged with many multinational companies in the field of international real estate investment, communication, technology, diamond, gold, mining, Pre-Feb housing, wind & solar energy, outsourcing management, and project consulting along with business partners & associates worldwide. Mr. Bakht has participated in major national and international conferences including participated in United Nations (U.N.O.) conferences.

TRAVEL: Mr. Bakht is well-traveled and has visited many countries worldwide.

MANAGEMENT EXPERIENCE: Thirty-Six years of diversified experience in project consulting, marketing, and business management. As a Director of Marketing, Director of Public Relations, Director of International Affairs, Executive Vice President, President, CEO, and Chairman of many national & multinational companies. Mr. Bakht hired and trained many professionals as business consultants in international marketing and supervised them.

CERTIFICATE OF ACHIEVEMENT: Achievement Award was presented to Mr. Bakht by Stephen Fossler for five years of continued growth and customer satisfaction from 1996-to 2001.

HONORS MEMBER: Madison Who's Who of Professionals, having demonstrated exemplary achievement and distinguished contributions to the business community, registered at the Library of Congress in Washington D.C. USA. (2007 & 2008)

HONORS MEMBER: Premiere who's Who International, professional business executive having demonstrated exemplary achievement and distinguished contributions to the International business community, 2008 and 2009.

CERTIFICATES: Certificate of Authenticity from Bill Rodham Clinton, President of the United States, and Hillary Rodham Clinton First Lady, USA. (July 20, 2000);

CERTIFICATE OF AUTHENTICITY: from Terence R. McAuliffe, Chairman of Democratic National Committee, Tom Dachle, Senate Democratic Leader, Dick Gephardt, House Democratic Leader, USA. (June 16, 2001);

CERTIFICATE OF AUTHENTICITY: from Terence R. McAuliffe, Chairman of Democratic National Committee, USA. (April 16, 2002).

CHAPTER 1

Introduction

Business and finance are crucial elements that drive modern society. They are deeply connected and play vital roles in various aspects of daily life and the economy. Business involves any activity related to the production or sale of goods and services with the goal of making a profit. This can range from individual entrepreneurs and small businesses to large multinational corporations.

Finance, on the other hand, involves managing money and assets, which includes investments, loans, and the planning of income and expenditures. It's all about ensuring that financial resources are used wisely and effectively to help organizations meet their goals.

The relationship between business and finance is symbiotic. Businesses need finance to grow and operate, while financial systems rely on successful businesses to generate profits and returns. Understanding both fields is crucial for anyone looking to start a business or work in finance, as they provide the foundation for economic stability and growth.

The concept of business has been around since ancient times, with trade and commerce being integral to early civilizations like the Greeks and Romans. Over centuries, business practices have evolved significantly, leading to the establishment of banks, stock markets, and complex corporate structures.

Finance as a distinct area of study emerged in the early 20th century, moving beyond basic money management to address the complexities of growing financial markets and new investment opportunities. This led to the development of specialized academic programs in finance, which now cover extensive topics such as corporate finance, investment strategies, financial markets, and risk management.

Understanding the history and development of business and finance helps in appreciating their impact on today's world. It highlights how both fields have adapted to meet the needs of increasingly complex economic environments, helping individuals and companies to not only survive but thrive.

Definition of Business and Finance

Business and finance are two interconnected fields crucial for the smooth functioning of modern society. Business encompasses a broad range of activities where individuals and organizations engage in commercial, industrial, or professional pursuits aimed at generating profits. This includes everything from small sole proprietorships to large corporations across diverse industries like manufacturing, retail, hospitality, and services.

Finance, as described by the Financial Times, involves managing substantial sums of money, primarily by large companies or governments. This management includes the allocation of financial resources through activities such as investing, borrowing, lending, and budgeting. The goal is to use these resources efficiently to meet the objectives of the organization.

The relationship between business and finance is symbiotic. Businesses need financial management to thrive and expand, while financial systems rely on successful business operations to generate economic returns. The field of finance itself is broad, covering financial planning, investment management, risk management, and corporate finance. Professionals in finance play a crucial role in allocating resources wisely, identifying risks and opportunities, and offering strategic advice to management teams.

Together, business and finance form a dynamic part of the economy, driving the creation of wealth and effective resource management. These fields are foundational to economic growth and are essential for anyone involved in managing or establishing a business.

Importance of Business and Finance in the modern world

Business and finance are integral to modern society, propelling economic growth, creating jobs, and equipping individuals and organizations with the tools to achieve their objectives. These fields are vital across various domains such as entrepreneurship, economic development, and investment.

Starting new ventures is financially demanding, requiring substantial initial investments, marketing, and product development funds. Without accessible capital, potential entrepreneurs might find it impossible to launch their projects, limiting innovation and job creation in the economy.

As companies grow, they frequently need more staff, significantly boosting employment, especially in developing countries where new job opportunities can dramatically improve living standards.

Investments play a critical role by supplying the capital necessary for businesses to expand and innovate. This supports not only economic growth but also the development of solutions to global challenges like climate change and public health.

16

The expansion of businesses directly contributes to economic development, creating wealth and improving quality of life. This progress leads to advancements in education, healthcare, and technology.

The financial sector, including banking and other financial services, is crucial, offering loans, credit, and essential services needed for daily operations. This support helps businesses manage cash flow challenges, purchase new equipment, or develop innovative products.

Furthermore, business and finance are key in developing and maintaining infrastructure like transport networks and energy facilities. Such investments enhance a region's economic efficiency and competitiveness while addressing global issues such as environmental sustainability.

The advancement of sectors such as renewable energy, biotechnology, and information technology relies heavily on financial investment. These industries are essential for addressing global challenges and improving global living standards.

The influence of business and finance spans multiple facets of society, enhancing economic performance and contributing to the well-being of communities worldwide. Understanding these fields is crucial for anyone aiming to make a significant impact, from banking and entrepreneurship to policy-making and beyond.

CHAPTER 2

The Dynamics of Business and Finance

A business is an organization or enterprise engaged in commercial, industrial, or professional activities with the aim of generating revenue, profit, or income. The main purpose of a business is to provide goods or services to customers in exchange for money or other forms of compensation.

Businesses can take many forms, such as sole proprietorships, partnerships, corporations, and cooperatives, and can operate in various industries such as manufacturing, finance, technology, healthcare, and many more. A business may also be involved in activities such as marketing, sales, human resources, finance, and management.

Successful businesses are typically those that have a clear understanding of their target market, their customers' needs and preferences, and how to provide a product or service that meets those needs in a profitable way. They also need to manage their resources effectively and efficiently to maximize their profits and achieve long-term sustainability.

At its core, a business is an organization that provides goods or services to customers with the aim of generating revenue or profit. This can be done through a variety of means, such as selling products directly to consumers, providing professional services, or offering goods or services to other businesses.

A business can take many forms, depending on its legal structure and ownership. The most common types of businesses are:

- ❖ **Sole Proprietorship**: This is a business owned and operated by one person. The owner is responsible for all aspects of the business, including its debts and liabilities.
- ❖ **Partnership**: A partnership is a business owned by two or more people. The partners share the profits and losses of the business, as well as its debts and liabilities.
- ❖ **Corporation**: A corporation is a legal entity that is separate from its owners. It is owned by shareholders, who elect a board of directors to manage the business.

❖ **Limited Liability Company (LLC):** An LLC is a hybrid of a corporation and a partnership. It provides limited liability protection to its owners, while still allowing them to participate in the management of the business.

Structure	Ownership	Liability	Taxes	Best For
Sole Proprietorship	One person	Personal responsibility for debts	Owner's personal tax	Freelancers, small ventures
Partnership	2+ people	Shared personal liability	Partners' personal taxes	Family businesses
Corporation	Shareholders	No personal liability	Corporate taxes	Large companies
LLC	Members	No personal liability	Members' personal taxes	Small to medium businesses

A successful business requires a clear understanding of its target market, the needs and preferences of its customers, and how to provide a product or service that meets those needs in a profitable way. This requires market research, product development, and effective marketing and sales strategies. To providing goods or services to customers, businesses must also manage their resources effectively to maximize profits and achieve long-term sustainability. This includes managing finances, human resources, operations, and supply chains.

Businesses also have a social responsibility to operate in an ethical and sustainable manner. This includes complying with laws and regulations, treating employees fairly, and minimizing the impact of their operations on the environment. A business is an organization that provides goods or services to customers with the aim of generating revenue or profit. Successful businesses require a clear understanding of their target market, effective management of resources, and a commitment to ethical and sustainable practices.

Businesses come in all shapes and sizes, and the specific type of business structure that an entrepreneur chooses can have significant implications for issues such as liability, taxes, management, and funding. The most common types of businesses include sole proprietorships, partnerships; limited liability companies (LLCs), corporations, and cooperatives. Each of these business structures has its own unique characteristics, advantages, and disadvantages.

Sole Proprietorship

A sole proprietorship is the simplest and most common form of business. It is a business that is owned and operated by a single individual who assumes all of the business's debts and liabilities. Sole proprietorships are popular among small business owners who want to have complete control over their business and keep their operations simple.

Advantages	Disadvantages
• Easy and inexpensive to set up • Owner has complete control over business decisions • All profits go directly to the owner • Minimal regulation and reporting requirements	• Owner is personally liable for business debts and liabilities • Limited access to funding • Business does not have a separate legal identity, which can make it difficult to sell or transfer ownership • Limited opportunities for tax planning

Partnership

A partnership is a business structure in which two or more individuals own and operate a business together. Partnerships can be general partnerships or limited partnerships, and each type of partnership has its own unique characteristics. In a general partnership, all partners share equal responsibility for the management and finances of the business. In a limited partnership, there are both general partners, who manage the business, and limited partners, who invest in the business but do not have a say in management decisions.

Advantages	Disadvantages
• Easy and inexpensive to set up • Partners can pool their resources and skills • Partners share the workload and decision-making responsibilities • More access to funding than a sole proprietorship	• Partners are jointly and severally liable for business debts and liabilities • Disagreements between partners can lead to conflicts • Limited opportunities for tax planning

Limited Liability Company (LLC)

A limited liability company (LLC) is a hybrid business structure that combines the flexibility and tax benefits of a partnership with the liability protection of a corporation. An LLC is a separate legal entity from its owners, and the owners are not personally liable for the company's debts and liabilities. LLCs can have one or more owners, known as members.

Advantages	Disadvantages
• Owners are not personally liable for business debts and liabilities • Flexible management structure • More access to funding than a sole proprietorship or partnership • Opportunity for tax planning	• More complex and expensive to set up than a sole proprietorship or partnership • LLCs must follow more regulation and reporting requirements than sole proprietorships and partnerships • Ownership transfer can be more difficult than a corporation • Some states do not recognize LLCs

Corporation

A corporation is a legal entity that is separate from its owners. A corporation can have many shareholders, who elect a board of directors to make management decisions on their behalf. Shareholders are not personally liable for the company's debts and liabilities.

Advantages	Disadvantages
• Owners are not personally liable for business debts and liabilities • Unlimited lifespan • Easier to raise large amounts of capital • Opportunity for tax planning	• More complex and expensive to set up and maintain than other business structures • Greater regulation and reporting requirements • Double taxation of profits • Ownership transfer can be difficult

Franchise

A franchise is a business model in which a franchisor grants the right to use its business name, products, and processes to a franchisee in exchange for payment of fees and royalties. Franchisees are responsible for running the business according to the franchisor's guidelines.

Advantages	Disadvantages
• Established brand and marketing • Access to proven business processes • Support from the franchisor	• High upfront costs to purchase the franchise • Ongoing fees and royalties • Limited control over business decisions

Nonprofit Organization

A nonprofit organization is a business that exists to serve a social or charitable purpose, rather than to make a profit. Nonprofits are exempt from federal income taxes, and donations to nonprofits are tax-deductible.

Advantages	Disadvantage
• Opportunity to make a positive impact on society • Exempt from federal income taxes • Donations are tax-deductible	• Limited access to funding • More complex and expensive to set up and maintain than other business structures • Limited ability to compensate employees

Joint Venture

A joint venture is a business arrangement in which two or more parties agree to contribute resources to a specific project or business initiative. Joint ventures can be formed for a specific period of time or for a specific purpose.

Advantages	Disadvantages
• Access to additional resources and expertise • Shared risk and reward	• Potential for disagreements and conflicts • Limited control over the joint

• Opportunity to enter new markets	venture

Holding Company

A holding company is a business that owns other businesses, but does not necessarily operate them. The purpose of a holding company is often to control the assets and investments of the subsidiary businesses.

Advantages	Disadvantages
• Limited liability for the holding company • Ability to control and manage multiple businesses • Potential for tax benefits	• More complex and expensive to set up and maintain than other business structures • Limited ability to generate revenue on its own • Potential for conflicts with subsidiary businesses

Social Enterprise

A social enterprise is a business that exists to achieve a social or environmental goal, while also generating revenue. Social enterprises can take many forms, including non-profits, cooperatives, and LLCs.

Advantages	Disadvantages
• Opportunity to make a positive impact on society or the environment • Potential for tax benefits • Access to funding and support from social impact investors.	• Limited access to funding • More complex and expensive to set up and maintain than a traditional business • Balancing the social and financial goals of the enterprise can be challenging.

The type of business structure that an entrepreneur chooses depends on many factors, including personal preferences, liability concerns, funding needs, and tax considerations. Each type of business structure has its own unique characteristics, advantages, and disadvantages. Entrepreneurs should carefully consider all of their options before deciding on a business structure, and seek professional advice if necessary.

How to start a business

Starting a business can be a challenging and rewarding experience. It requires careful planning, research, and preparation to ensure that the business is successful in the long term. Here are the steps to follow to start a business:

Develop a Business Idea

The first step in starting a business is to come up with a business idea. This idea should be something that you are passionate about, that you have experience in, or that you believe will fill a need in the market. You can brainstorm ideas by identifying problems or needs that you see in your community or industry, or by considering your own skills and interests. Once you have a business idea, you should research the market to determine if there is a demand for your product or service.

Conduct Market Research

Market research is the process of gathering and analyzing information about your potential customers and competitors. It helps you determine if there is a demand for your product or service, what your competitors are doing, and what your target customers are willing to pay for your product or service. You can conduct market research by using surveys, focus groups, and online research tools. It is important to analyze the results of your research carefully to make informed decisions about your business.

Choose a Business Structure

Choosing a business structure is an important decision because it affects how your business will be taxed and how you will be personally liable for the business. The most common business structures are sole proprietorship, partnership, limited liability company (LLC), and corporation. Each structure has its own advantages and disadvantages. You should consult with a lawyer or accountant to determine the best structure for your business.

Write a Business Plan

A business plan is a roadmap for your business. It outlines your goals, strategies, and financial projections. A business plan should include an executive summary's, a company description, a market analysis, a marketing and sales plan, a product or service description, a financial plan, and a management and operations plan. A business plan helps you organize your thoughts, secure funding, and communicate your ideas to others. You can use a business plan template or hire a professional to write a business plan.

Register Your Business

Once you have chosen a business structure, you need to register your business with the government. This process varies depending on your location and business structure. You may need to register your business with the Secretary of State, obtain a business license, and register for taxes. You should consult with a lawyer or accountant to ensure that you are complying with all local and state regulations.

Starting a business often requires capital to cover expenses such as equipment, inventory, and marketing. There are many sources of funding available, including personal savings, loans from family and friends, crowdfunding, small business loans, and grants. You should research and compare the different funding options to determine the best one for your business.

Setting up your business operations includes finding a location, purchasing equipment and supplies, hiring employees, and setting up your accounting and record-keeping systems. You should create a checklist of tasks to ensure that you have everything you need to start your business.

Once you have completed all of the previous steps, it is time to launch your business. This includes promoting your business through advertising and marketing, setting up a website and social media accounts, and holding a launch event. You should track your results and adjust your strategies as necessary.

Managing your business is an ongoing process that involves monitoring your finances, tracking your sales and expenses, and making strategic decisions to grow your business. You should regularly review your business plan, assess your progress, and make changes as necessary.

Your business is only as strong as the people who run it. Hiring the right team can make or break your business. When building your team, look for people who are passionate, knowledgeable, and have skills that complement your own. You should also consider their values and work ethic, as they will play a significant role in shaping your company culture.

Your brand is the image and identity of your business. It is how your customers will perceive your company and what sets you apart from your competitors. Establishing your brand involves creating a memorable logo, developing a unique brand voice and messaging, and consistently using these elements across all marketing materials. You should also consider creating a brand style guide to ensure consistency in all branding efforts.

Develop a Marketing Strategy

Marketing is the process of promoting your business and products to your target audience. Developing a marketing strategy involves identifying your target audience, selecting the appropriate marketing channels, and creating a marketing plan that outlines your goals, budget, and tactics. You can use a variety of marketing channels, such as social media, email marketing, content marketing, and paid advertising.

Technology plays a significant role in modern business. Embracing technology can help you streamline your processes, increase efficiency, and improve communication with customers and employees. You should consider implementing technology solutions such as customer relationship management (CRM) software, project management tools, and accounting software to help you run your business more effectively.

As a business owner, it is important to stay compliant with all relevant regulations and laws. This includes local, state, and federal regulations related to taxes, employment, and environmental standards. You should consult with a lawyer or accountant to ensure that you are complying with all regulations.

Monitoring your finances is critical to the success of your business. You should track your expenses and revenue, create a budget, and regularly review your financial statements. This will help you identify areas where you can reduce expenses and increase revenue.

Starting a business is a complex process, but by following these steps, you can increase your chances of success. It is important to be patient, persistent, and adaptable, as the business landscape is constantly changing. With dedication and hard work, you can turn your business idea into a thriving venture.

Business planning and strategy are essential components of any successful business. A solid plan and strategy can help you define your goals, assess your resources, and determine the best way to achieve your objectives. In this article, we'll explore the key steps involved in business planning and strategy.

The first step in business planning and strategy is to define your vision and mission. Your vision is the long-term goal for your business, while your mission is the purpose and values that guide your business. To create a vision and mission statement, consider what you want to achieve with your business, what your core values are, and what sets you apart from your competitors.

Once you have defined your vision and mission, it's time to conduct a SWOT analysis. SWOT stands for strengths, weaknesses, opportunities, and threats. This analysis will help you identify your strengths and weaknesses, as well as potential opportunities and threats in the market.

After conducting a SWOT analysis, you can set SMART goals. SMART goals are specific, measurable, achievable, relevant, and time-bound. This will help you focus your efforts on achieving your most important objectives.

To be successful, you must understand your target market. This involves identifying who your ideal customers are, their needs and wants, and where they can be found. By doing so, you can tailor your marketing and sales efforts to meet their specific needs and preferences.

Your unique selling proposition (USP) is what sets you apart from your competitors. It's the reason why customers choose your products or services over others. To develop your USP, consider what makes your business unique and what value you offer to your customers.

A marketing strategy is essential to promote your products or services to your target market. Your marketing strategy should be based on your USP, target market, and budget. It should also include tactics such as advertising, social media marketing, and content marketing.

A sales plan is essential to achieve your revenue goals. This involves setting sales targets, creating a sales process, and developing a sales team. It's important to track your progress regularly and adjust your sales plan as needed.

An operations plan outlines the day-to-day operations of your business. This includes how you will produce and deliver your products or services, as well as how you will manage your inventory, suppliers, and customer support.

A financial plan is essential to track and manage your business finances. This involves creating a budget, forecasting your revenue and expenses, and identifying your funding sources. It's important to track your financial performance regularly and adjust your financial plan as needed.

Monitoring and evaluating your plan is essential to ensure that you are on track to achieving your goals. This involves regularly reviewing your progress, analyzing your results, and adjusting your plan as needed.

Business planning and strategy are essential to the success of any business. By defining your vision and mission, conducting a SWOT analysis, setting SMART goals, identifying your target market, and developing a unique selling proposition, you can create a strong foundation for your business. Creating a marketing strategy, sales plan, operations plan, and financial plan, and monitoring and evaluating your plan, will help you achieve your objectives and grow your business.

Market research

Market research is the process of gathering and analyzing information about a market, including its size, competitors, and customer needs and preferences. Market research is an essential component of business strategy, as it provides insights into the market that businesses can use to make informed decisions.

Here are the key reasons why market research is important for businesses:

Market research helps businesses identify market opportunities, including untapped niches and emerging trends. By analyzing the market, businesses can develop products and services that meet customer needs and preferences, and differentiate themselves from their competitors.

Market research helps businesses understand the needs and preferences of their target customers. By gathering information about their customers' buying behavior, preferences, and attitudes, businesses can develop products and services that meet their customers' needs and preferences.

Market research helps businesses assess their competitors and develop strategies to differentiate themselves from their competitors. By analyzing their competitors' strengths and weaknesses, businesses can develop a competitive advantage and position themselves in the market.

Market research helps businesses evaluate the effectiveness of their marketing strategies. By gathering information about customer responses to marketing messages and advertising campaigns, businesses can refine their marketing strategies and improve their return on investment.

Market research helps businesses forecast sales and revenue. By analyzing the market, businesses can identify trends and forecast future demand for their products and services, which can help them, plan production, inventory, and pricing.

Market research helps businesses minimize risk by providing information that can inform business decisions. By analyzing market trends and customer behavior, businesses can make informed decisions about product development, marketing strategies, and pricing, which can minimize the risk of failure.

Market research is an essential component of business strategy. By gathering and analyzing information about the market, businesses can identify market opportunities, understand customer needs and preferences, assess competitors, evaluate marketing strategies, forecast sales and revenue, and minimize risk. By using market research to inform their decisions, businesses can increase their chances of success and achieve their objectives.

CHAPTER 3

Financial Statements

Financial statements are the reports that provide a comprehensive overview of a company's financial performance and position. They are critical tools for businesses to understand their financial health and to communicate their financial performance to stakeholders. In this article, we will provide an overview of the three main financial statements: the income statement, the balance sheet, and the cash flow statement.

Income Statement

The income statement, also known as the profit and loss statement, shows the company's revenues and expenses over a specific period of time, usually a quarter or a year. The income statement provides information about a company's profitability and can help investors and creditors assess the company's financial performance.

The income statement includes the following components:

- ❖ **Revenues:** This is the money a company earned from sales of products or services.
- ❖ **Cost of goods sold:** This is the cost of the products or services sold by the company.
- ❖ **Gross profit:** This is the difference between the revenues and the cost of goods sold.
- ❖ **Operating expenses**: These are the expenses incurred by the company to run its operations, such as rent, utilities, and salaries.
- ❖ **Operating income**: This is the difference between the gross profit and the operating expenses.
- ❖ **Other income and expenses**: These are non-operating items that can impact a company's net income, such as interest income or expenses.
- ❖ **Net income:** This is the company's total profit after all expenses have been deducted.

Balance Sheet

The balance sheet provides a snapshot of a company's financial position at a specific point in time. It shows what the company owns, what it owes, and what it is worth. The balance sheet can help investors and creditors assess the company's financial position and liquidity.

The balance sheet includes the following components:

- ❖ **Assets:** These are the things that the company owns, such as cash, inventory, and property.
- ❖ **Liabilities:** These are the things that the company owes, such as loans, accounts payable, and taxes.
- ❖ **Shareholders' equity:** This is the difference between the assets and liabilities, and represents the net worth of the company.

Cash Flow Statement

The cash flow statement provides information about a company's cash inflows and outflows over a specific period of time. It shows how much cash the company generated or used during the period, and provides insights into the company's liquidity and ability to meet its obligations.

The cash flow statement includes the following components:

- ❖ **Operating activities:** This includes cash flows from the company's primary operations, such as cash received from customers and cash paid to suppliers.
- ❖ **Investing activities:** This includes cash flows from the buying and selling of assets, such as property or investments.
- ❖ **Financing activities:** This includes cash flows from the company's financing activities, such as borrowing money or issuing shares.
- ❖ **Net cash flow:** This is the difference between the cash inflows and outflows during the period.

Financial statements can be used to analyze a company's financial performance and position. For example, by analyzing the income statement, an investor can see if the company is profitable and if it is generating enough revenue to cover its expenses. By analyzing the balance sheet, an investor can see if the company has a healthy financial position and if it has enough assets to cover its liabilities. By analyzing the cash flow statement, an investor can see if the company is generating enough cash to meet its obligations.

To these three main financial statements, companies may also prepare additional financial reports to provide further information about their financial performance and position. For example, companies may prepare a statement of changes in equity, which shows how the company's equity has changed over a specific period of time. Companies may also prepare notes to the financial statements, which provide additional information about the company's financial performance and position.

Importance of financial statements for businesses

Financial statements are an essential tool for businesses, investors, and other stakeholders to understand a company's financial performance and make informed decisions. These statements provide critical information about a company's financial health, including its revenues, expenses, assets, liabilities, and cash flows. In this article, we will discuss the importance of financial statements for businesses and their stakeholders.

Financial statements are an essential tool for business decision-making. Business owners, managers, and investors rely on financial statements to evaluate the financial performance of a company and make informed decisions about its future. Financial statements provide a clear and concise view of a company's current financial position, its profitability, and its liquidity. This information can help business owners make strategic decisions about investments, cost-cutting measures, expansion plans, and other important business decisions.

Financial statements are also critical for maintaining positive relationships with investors. Investors use financial statements to evaluate a company's financial health, and to determine whether to invest or divest in a particular company. Financial statements provide an objective and accurate view of a company's financial performance, and are a key tool for investors in evaluating a company's potential for long-term success.

Financial statements are a legal requirement for businesses in many jurisdictions. Publicly traded companies are required to file financial statements with regulatory bodies such as the Securities and Exchange Commission (SEC) in the United States. These statements are used to ensure that companies are complying with legal and regulatory requirements, including accounting standards, tax laws, and securities regulations.

Financial statements can also help businesses plan for the future by providing valuable information for budgeting and forecasting. By analyzing past financial statements, business owners and managers can identify trends in revenue, expenses, and profitability. This information can be used to make accurate predictions about future performance, and to create realistic budgets and forecasts for the company.

Financial statements are an important tool for internal control and risk management. By regularly reviewing financial statements, business owners and managers can identify areas of risk and take action to mitigate these risks. For example, a company may identify a pattern of increasing expenses, which may indicate that the company needs to take measures to control costs and improve profitability.

Financial statements can be used for benchmarking, which is the process of comparing a company's financial performance to that of other companies in the same industry. By comparing financial ratios, such as gross profit margin or return on equity, business owners and managers can identify areas of strength and weakness in their own company. This information can be used to improve performance and gain a competitive advantage.

CHAPTER 4

Financial Management

Financial management is the process of managing an organization's financial resources to achieve its goals and objectives. It involves planning, budgeting, accounting, reporting, and analysis of financial data. The goal of financial management is to optimize the use of financial resources to maximize profitability and ensure the long-term financial health of the organization. In this article, we will discuss the key components of financial management and their importance for businesses.

Financial planning and budgeting

Financial planning and budgeting are two critical components of financial management. They involve the process of analyzing an organization's financial situation, identifying goals, and developing a plan for allocating resources in the most efficient and effective way to achieve those goals. In this article, we will discuss financial planning and budgeting, their importance for businesses, and best practices for developing a financial plan and budget.

Financial Planning

Financial planning is the process of identifying an organization's financial goals and developing a plan to achieve them. The process involves analyzing the organization's financial resources, assessing its financial needs, and developing a budget to allocate those resources in the most efficient and effective way.

The first step in financial planning is to identify the organization's financial goals. These goals can include increasing revenue, reducing costs, improving profitability, or expanding operations. Once the goals have been identified, the

organization must assess its financial situation, including its current assets, liabilities, and cash flow. This assessment will help the organization understand its financial resources and identify any financial constraints that may affect its ability to achieve its goals.

Once the organization has assessed its financial situation, it can begin developing a financial plan. The financial plan should outline the steps the organization will take to achieve its financial goals. It should also identify any risks or challenges that may impact the organization's ability to achieve its goals and outline strategies for mitigating those risks.

Budgeting

Budgeting is the process of creating a financial plan for a specific period, usually a year. It involves estimating revenues and expenses for the period and allocating resources to achieve the organization's goals and objectives. Budgeting is an important tool for financial management as it provides a framework for decision-making, helps to control costs, and ensures that resources are allocated in the most effective and efficient way.

The first step in budgeting is to estimate the organization's revenue for the period. This can include revenue from sales, investments, and other sources. The organization must also estimate its expenses for the period, including the cost of goods sold, salaries and wages, rent, utilities, and other expenses. The difference between the revenue and expenses is the organization's net income.

Once the organization has estimated its revenue and expenses, it can begin allocating resources to achieve its goals. This involves prioritizing expenses and identifying areas where resources can be reallocated to achieve the greatest impact. The organization should also develop a contingency plan to address unexpected expenses or changes in the business environment.

Importance of Financial Planning and Budgeting

Financial planning and budgeting are critical for businesses for several reasons. First, they help businesses achieve their financial goals by providing a roadmap for resource allocation. Second, they help businesses identify and manage financial risks, which can impact the organization's ability to achieve its goals. Third, financial planning and budgeting help businesses control costs and manage cash flow, which is essential for financial stability and growth.

Best Practices for Financial Planning and Budgeting

There are several best practices for developing a financial plan and budget. These include:

- ❖ **Set realistic goals:** The organization's financial goals should be achievable and realistic. Setting unrealistic goals can lead to frustration and a lack of motivation.
- ❖ **Involve all stakeholders:** The financial plan and budget should be developed with input from all stakeholders, including senior management, department managers, and other key employees.
- ❖ **Use historical data**: Historical data can provide insight into past performance and help organizations develop more accurate revenue and expense estimates.
- ❖ **Monitor performance:** The financial plan and budget should be regularly monitored and adjusted as needed to ensure that the organization is on track to achieve its goals.
- ❖ **Develop a contingency plan:** A contingency plan should be developed to address unexpected expenses or changes in the business environment.

Financial analysis and decision-making are essential aspects of running a successful business. Financial analysis is the process of examining an organization's financial information to make informed decisions about its financial health and future. Financial decision-making is the process of using financial information to make decisions that affect the organization's operations, investments, and overall financial stability. In this article, we will discuss financial analysis and decision-making, their importance, and best practices for analyzing financial data and making informed decisions.

Financial analysis is the process of examining an organization's financial statements to understand its financial health, trends, and future prospects. The analysis includes reviewing financial statements such as the income statement, balance sheet, and cash flow statement, as well as other financial data such as industry benchmarks, market trends, and economic indicators.

The purpose of financial analysis is to assess an organization's ability to generate revenue, manage expenses, and generate profits. The analysis helps to identify areas where the organization can improve its financial performance and make informed decisions about its operations and investments.

Some of the key financial ratios used in financial analysis include:

- **Liquidity ratios:** Measures the organization's ability to meet its short-term obligations. Examples include the current ratio, quick ratio, and working capital ratio.
- **Profitability ratios:** Measures the organization's ability to generate profits. Examples include gross profit margin, net profit margin, and return on investment.
- **Efficiency ratios**: Measures the organization's ability to manage its assets and liabilities. Examples include inventory turnover, accounts receivable turnover, and accounts payable turnover.
- **Leverage ratios**: Measures the organization's use of debt and its ability to meet its long-term obligations. Examples include debt-to-equity ratio, interest coverage ratio, and debt-to-assets ratio.

Financial Decision-Making

Financial decision-making is the process of using financial information to make informed decisions about the organization's operations, investments, and overall financial stability. The decisions can include capital investments, financing, mergers and acquisitions, dividend policy, and other financial decisions that impact the organization's financial performance.

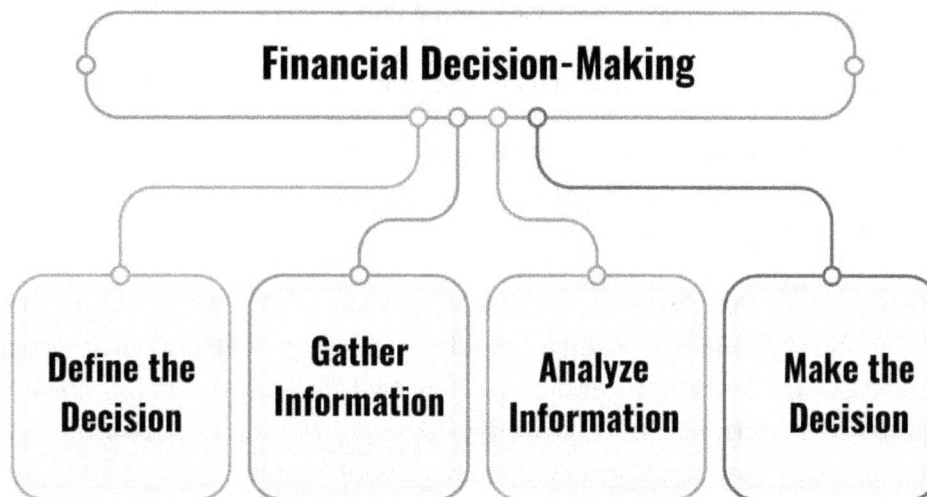

```
            Financial Decision-Making

  Define the    Gather      Analyze      Make the
  Decision      Information  Information  Decision
```

The financial decision-making process involves several steps, including:

- **Defining the decision**: The first step is to define the decision and the goals of the decision. This may involve assessing the organization's financial health, identifying potential investments, or evaluating financing options.
- **Gathering information:** The next step is to gather financial information to inform the decision. This may involve analyzing financial statements, market data, industry trends, and other financial data.
- **Analyzing the information:** The third step is to analyze the financial data and assess the financial impact of different decisions. This may involve using financial models, performing sensitivity analysis, or assessing risk.
- **Making the decision:** The final step is to make the decision based on the financial analysis and other factors such as strategic objectives, risk tolerance, and stakeholder preferences.

Importance of Financial Analysis and Decision-Making

Financial analysis and decision-making are essential for businesses for several reasons. First, financial analysis provides insights into the organization's financial health and future prospects. This information helps the organization make informed decisions about its operations, investments, and financial stability.

Second, financial decision-making helps the organization allocate resources effectively and efficiently. This improves the organization's financial performance and ensures that resources are used to achieve the organization's goals.

Third, financial analysis and decision-making help the organization manage financial risks. The analysis helps to identify potential risks, while decision-making helps the organization develop strategies to mitigate those risks.

Best Practices for Financial Analysis and Decision-Making

There are several best practices for financial analysis and decision-making, including

Use accurate and reliable financial data: The financial analysis and decision-making process rely on accurate and reliable financial data. The organization should ensure that its financial data is complete, accurate, and up-to-date.

Risk management and insurance are critical components of business management. Risk management involves identifying, assessing, and mitigating potential risks that could affect a business's operations or finances. Insurance is a tool that businesses use to transfer risks to an insurance company. In this article, we will discuss the importance of risk management and insurance for businesses, key concepts in risk management, and best practices for implementing a risk management and insurance program.

Businesses face many risks that could impact their operations, finances, or reputation. These risks include natural disasters, cyber-attacks, lawsuits, and supply chain disruptions, among others. Risk management is essential for businesses to identify and mitigate these risks to protect their assets, minimize financial losses, and maintain their reputation.

Insurance is an essential tool for businesses to transfer risks to an insurance company. By paying a premium, a business can transfer the risk of a potential loss to the insurance company. If the loss occurs, the insurance company will cover the cost, subject to the policy's terms and conditions.

Key Concepts in Risk Management

There are several key concepts in risk management that businesses should be aware of. These include:

- ✓ **Risk identification:** This involves identifying potential risks that could impact the business. Risks can come from a variety of sources, including natural disasters, cyber-attacks, supply chain disruptions, and employee errors.
- ✓ **Risk assessment:** Once risks are identified, they need to be assessed to determine the likelihood and potential impact of the risk. This helps businesses prioritize risks and allocate resources to address the most significant risks.

- ✓ **Risk mitigation**: This involves taking steps to reduce the likelihood or impact of a potential risk. Mitigation strategies can include implementing security measures, developing contingency plans, and purchasing insurance.
- ✓ **Risk transfer:** This involves transferring the risk of a potential loss to another party, such as an insurance company.

Best Practices for Implementing a Risk Management and Insurance Program:

Implementing a risk management and insurance program requires a systematic approach. The following are some best practices for businesses to consider when implementing a risk management and insurance program:

Identify and assess risks: The first step in developing a risk management program is to identify and assess potential risks. Businesses should review their operations, supply chain, and external factors that could impact their operations, such as natural disasters or cyber-attacks.

Develop a risk management plan: Once risks are identified, businesses should develop a risk management plan that outlines how they will mitigate or transfer each risk. The plan should include strategies to minimize the likelihood and impact of potential risks.

Implement security measures: Businesses should implement security measures to reduce the likelihood of cyber-attacks or data breaches. These measures can include firewalls, antivirus software, and employee training on security best practices.

Develop contingency plans: Businesses should develop contingency plans to respond to potential risks, such as natural disasters or supply chain disruptions. Contingency plans should include procedures for communicating with employees, customers, and suppliers.

Purchase insurance: Businesses should purchase insurance to transfer the risk of potential losses to an insurance company. The insurance policy should cover the specific risks that the business faces, and the business should review the policy's terms and conditions carefully.

Review and update the risk management program: Businesses should regularly review and update their risk management program to reflect changes in their operations, external factors, or new risks that emerge.

Investments and asset management

Investments and asset management are critical components of financial planning and management for individuals and businesses alike. Investments are assets that generate income or appreciate in value, while asset management involves managing and optimizing the performance of these assets. In this article, we will discuss the importance of investments and asset management, key concepts in investment and asset management, and best practices for implementing an investment and asset management program.

Investments are critical for individuals and businesses to achieve their financial goals, such as saving for retirement, funding education, or growing a business. Investments can generate income through interest or dividends, or appreciate in value through capital gains. However, investments also carry risks, such as market volatility and inflation that can impact their performance.

Asset management is essential for individuals and businesses to manage their investments and optimize their performance. Asset management involves selecting investments, monitoring their performance, and adjusting the investment mix to align with the investor's goals and risk tolerance.

Key Concepts in Investment and Asset Management

Asset allocation, diversification, risk management, performance monitoring, and rebalancing are crucial elements of effective investment and asset management. Asset allocation involves distributing investments across various asset classes like stocks, bonds, and cash, playing a significant role in defining the risk and return of a portfolio. Diversification further mitigates risk by spreading investments within each asset class, reducing the impact of a single investment's performance on the overall portfolio. Risk management requires identifying potential investment risks and developing strategies to manage or transfer these risks. Monitoring performance ensures the investments align with the investor's goals and risk tolerance, while rebalancing adjusts the portfolio to maintain the desired asset allocation and risk levels.

When implementing an investment and asset management program, it's essential to follow a systematic approach. Start by identifying your investment goals, such as saving for retirement or funding a business. These goals will inform your investment choices and asset allocation strategy. Understanding your risk tolerance is also critical; it determines how much risk you're willing to accept and guides your investment decisions. After setting your goals and determining risk tolerance, choose investments that match your objectives and risk profile. Consider various options like stocks, bonds, mutual funds, and exchange-traded funds (ETFs). Once investments are selected, implement asset allocation and diversification strategies to optimize performance and manage risk.

Regular monitoring of your investments is necessary to ensure they continue to meet your financial goals. Adjust your investment mix as needed to maintain your desired asset allocation and risk profile. For those who lack the time or expertise, professional asset management services can offer customized investment strategies and ongoing portfolio management. Regular reviews and updates to your investment and asset management program are essential to accommodate any changes in your financial goals, risk tolerance, or market conditions. This dynamic approach ensures your investment strategy remains aligned with your long-term objectives, helping you navigate through various market scenarios effectively.

CHAPTER 5

Funding Your Business

Funding is a critical element of starting and growing a business. Whether an entrepreneur is launching a startup, expanding an existing business, or undertaking a new project, funding is necessary to cover costs, invest in growth, and generate returns. In this article, we will discuss the different types of funding options available to businesses, the pros and cons of each, and best practices for selecting and securing funding.

Types of Funding Options

There are several types of funding options available to businesses. These include:

Bootstrapping: This involves self-funding the business by using personal savings or credit, taking out loans, or using credit cards. Bootstrapping can be an effective way to launch a business without incurring debt or sacrificing equity.

Friends and Family: This involves borrowing from friends and family members who believe in the business's potential. Friends and family funding can be an affordable way to raise capital, but it can also create personal and emotional risks.

Crowdfunding: This involves raising funds from a large group of individuals through online platforms, such as Kickstarter or Indiegogo. Crowdfunding can be an effective way to test the market, generate buzz, and raise capital.

Angel Investors: This involves raising funds from individual investors who provide capital in exchange for equity or convertible debt. Angel investors can bring expertise, connections, and resources to the business, but they may also demand a high return on investment.

Venture Capital: This involves raising funds from venture capital firms that invest in high-growth startups in exchange for equity. Venture capital can provide significant capital and resources, but it can also involve giving up control and ownership of the business.

Bank Loans: This involves borrowing money from a bank or other financial institution in exchange for interest payments and collateral. Bank loans can be a reliable source of capital, but they often require significant documentation, collateral, and creditworthiness.

Grants: This involves applying for funding from government agencies, foundations, or other organizations that provide grants to support specific types of businesses or projects. Grants do not have to be repaid, but they can be highly competitive and require a significant amount of time and effort to secure.

Pros and Cons of Funding Options

Funding Type	Source	Pros	Cons
Bootstrapping	Personal savings, credit	Full control retained, no debt or equity sacrificed	Limited funds, personal financial risk
Friends and Family	Personal network	Low-cost capital, supportive investors	Potential personal and emotional risks
Crowdfunding	Online platforms	Market testing, buzz generation, no equity lost	Uncertain funding, requires significant marketing
Angel Investors	Individual investors	Capital plus expertise and network	Potential loss of control, high return expectations
Venture Capital	VC firms	Large capital amounts, valuable resources	Significant equity loss, possible loss of operational control
Bank Loans	Financial institutions	Reliable source of funds, structured repayment	Requires collateral, strict credit requirements
Grants	Governments, foundations	Non-repayable funds, support for specific projects	Highly competitive, complex application process

Sources of funding for businesses

Securing funding is crucial to the success of any business, regardless of its size or industry. There are various sources of funding that entrepreneurs can turn to when looking to raise capital for their businesses. In this article, we will discuss some of the most common sources of funding for businesses.

The most common source of funding for small businesses is personal savings. Entrepreneurs often use their own funds to start or grow their businesses, as this allows them to retain full control of the business and avoid the complexities of external funding sources. While personal savings can be a low-cost source of funding, it is also a high-risk option, as the entrepreneur's personal assets are at stake if the business fails.

Entrepreneurs can also turn to friends and family members for funding. This can be a good option for businesses that are just starting out and may not be able to secure funding from other sources. Friends and family members may be willing to lend money at a lower interest rate than traditional lenders, and may be more flexible in terms of repayment terms. However, borrowing from friends and family can put personal relationships at risk, especially if the business fails to generate returns.

Crowdfunding has become a popular funding source for small businesses and startups. Crowdfunding platforms allow entrepreneurs to pitch their business ideas to a large audience of potential investors, who can then contribute funds to the project. Crowdfunding can be a good option for businesses that are looking to raise a small amount of capital quickly, and can also provide a way to test the market and generate buzz for a new product or service. However, crowdfunding can be time-consuming and may not be suitable for all types of businesses.

Angel investors are high-net-worth individuals who provide funding to early-stage businesses in exchange for an equity stake. Angel investors typically invest smaller amounts of capital than venture capitalists, and can provide valuable mentorship and networking opportunities to entrepreneurs. However, angel investors typically expect high returns on their investments, and may require a significant amount of control over the business in exchange for their funding.

Venture capital (VC) is a type of financing that is typically provided to early-stage businesses with high growth potential. Venture capitalists invest in businesses in exchange for an equity stake, and can provide significant amounts of funding, often in the millions of dollars. Venture capitalists typically look for businesses that have a strong team, a unique product or service, and a large market opportunity. However, venture capitalists often require a high degree of control over the business and may put pressure on entrepreneurs to deliver returns quickly.

Traditional bank loans are a common source of funding for small businesses. Bank loans typically offer lower interest rates than other types of financing, and can be used for a variety of business purposes, such as purchasing inventory or equipment, or expanding the business. However, bank loans can be difficult to obtain, especially for new businesses or those with less-than-perfect credit. Banks typically require a significant amount of documentation, collateral, and a strong credit history to qualify for a loan.

The Small Business Administration (SBA) offers a variety of loan programs to help small businesses secure funding. SBA loans are backed by the federal government, which can make them a more attractive option for lenders, as they carry less risk. SBA loans can be used for a variety of purposes, including working capital, equipment purchases, and real estate. However, SBA loans can be difficult to obtain, as they require a significant amount of documentation and a strong credit history.

Equity financing is a method of raising capital for a business by selling shares of ownership in the company. In exchange for giving investors ownership rights in the company, the business receives the capital it needs to fund its operations, make investments, and grow.

There are several types of equity financing, including

Common stock: This is the most common type of equity financing, and it refers to the sale of shares of common stock to investors. Common stockholders have the right to vote on company decisions and to receive a portion of the company's profits in the form of dividends.

Preferred stock: Preferred stock is a type of stock that gives investors a higher priority when it comes to receiving dividends and distributions. Preferred stockholders do not have voting rights in the company.

Convertible debt: Convertible debt is a hybrid form of financing that starts out as debt but can be converted into equity at a later date. This type of financing is often used in early-stage startups, where investors are not yet ready to value the company and determine a price for its shares. Venture capital: Venture capital is a form of equity financing that is typically provided by institutional investors, such as venture capital firms, to early-stage companies with high growth potential. In exchange for the investment, the venture capitalist receives an ownership stake in the company.

Angel investing: Angel investors are high-net-worth individuals who invest in startups and small businesses. Unlike venture capitalists, angel investors typically invest smaller amounts of money and may be willing to take on more risk. Crowdfunding: Crowdfunding is a newer form of equity financing that has become increasingly popular in recent years. It involves raising capital from a large number of investors through an online platform. Crowdfunding can be used for a variety of purposes, including raising seed capital for a startup, funding a product launch, or financing a specific project.

Equity financing can be an attractive option for businesses that are looking to raise capital without taking on debt. By selling shares of ownership in the company, the business can access the funds it needs to grow and expand, while also sharing the risk and potential rewards with its investors. However, it is important to carefully consider the terms of any equity financing arrangement to ensure that the business is able to maintain control over its operations and strategy, and that it is not giving away too much equity too early in its development.

Debt financing

Debt financing is a method of raising capital for a business by borrowing money from investors or lenders, with the agreement to repay the borrowed funds with interest over a set period of time. This type of financing is often used by businesses to fund operational expenses, make capital investments, or finance expansion projects.

There are several types of debt financing, including:

Bank loans

These are loans made by banks or other financial institutions to businesses. Bank loans can be secured or unsecured, and they typically have a fixed interest rate and a set repayment schedule.

Lines of credit: A line of credit is a type of loan that provides a business with access to a pool of funds that can be borrowed as needed. Lines of credit are often used to fund short-term working capital needs, such as inventory purchases or payroll expenses. Asset-based lending: Asset-based lending is a type of loan that is secured by a business's assets, such as inventory, accounts receivable, or equipment. The amount of the loan is based on the value of the assets being used as collateral.

Bonds

 Bonds are a form of debt financing that are sold to investors in exchange for a promise to pay back the borrowed funds with interest over a set period of time. Bonds can be issued by companies or governments.

Factoring

 Factoring is a type of debt financing that involves selling a business's accounts receivable to a factoring company in exchange for immediate cash. The factoring company then collects the payments owed by the customers who owe the business money.

Merchant cash advances

 Merchant cash advances are a type of financing that provides a business with a lump sum of cash in exchange for a percentage of its future credit card sales. This type of financing can be expensive, as the interest rates are often much higher than traditional bank loans.

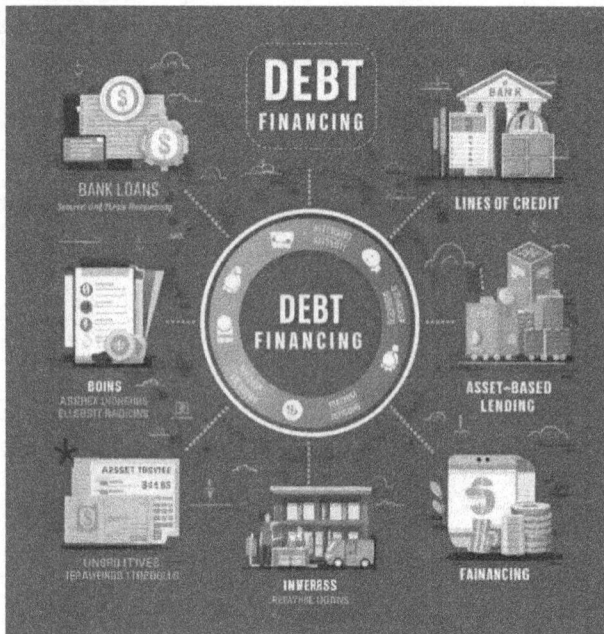

Debt financing can be an attractive option for businesses that need to raise capital quickly or that have a solid track record of revenue and profitability. Unlike equity financing, where the business gives up a portion of ownership in the company, debt financing allows the business to maintain full control over its operations and strategy. Additionally, interest paid on debt financing is tax-deductible, which can provide a significant benefit to the business. However, there are also potential downsides to debt financing. One of the main risks is the potential for default if the business is unable to make its scheduled loan payments. Defaulting on a loan can have serious consequences, including damage to the business's credit rating and possible legal action by the lender. Additionally, taking on too much debt can limit the business's ability to take on additional debt in the future, as lenders may be hesitant to lend to a business with high levels of outstanding debt.

When considering debt financing, it is important to carefully evaluate the terms of any loan or credit agreement to ensure that the business is able to meet its repayment obligations and that the interest rate and other fees are reasonable. It is also important to consider the impact that taking on debt will have on the business's overall financial health and long-term growth prospects.

Crowdfunding and alternative financing

Crowdfunding and alternative financing are relatively new methods of raising capital for businesses. These methods have become more popular in recent years due to their ease of use, accessibility, and ability to reach a large number of potential investors or lenders. In this article, we will discuss the different types of crowdfunding and alternative financing, and the advantages and disadvantages of using these methods for raising capital. Crowdfunding Crowdfunding is a method of raising capital from a large number of people, typically through an online platform. The idea is that many people will contribute small amounts of money to support a project or business, rather than a few people investing large sums. There are different types of crowdfunding, including:

Donation-based crowdfunding: This type of crowdfunding involves raising money through donations, with no expectation of financial return. This is often used for social causes or charitable organizations.

Reward-based crowdfunding: This type of crowdfunding involves offering a reward, such as a product or service, in exchange for a donation. This is commonly used by startups to raise money to develop a new product or service.

Equity-based crowdfunding: This type of crowdfunding involves selling shares in a business to a large number of investors. Investors receive a financial return based on the success of the business.

Advantages	Disadvantages
❖ Access to a large pool of potential investors or donors ❖ Quick and easy to set up a campaign on a crowdfunding platform ❖ No requirement for collateral or personal guarantees ❖ Can provide exposure and marketing opportunities for the business or project	❖ Can be time-consuming and labor-intensive to manage a crowdfunding campaign ❖ Crowdfunding platforms may take a percentage of the funds raised as a fee ❖ Equity-based crowdfunding may require significant legal and regulatory compliance ❖ Can be difficult to stand out among the many other crowdfunding campaigns on the platform

Alternative financing

Alternative financing refers to any method of raising capital that is outside of the traditional banking system. This can include:

Peer-to-peer lending: This involves borrowing money from individual investors, rather than a traditional bank. Peer-to-peer lending platforms connect borrowers with investors, who receive a return on their investment in the form of interest.

Invoice financing: This involves selling unpaid invoices to a financing company in exchange for immediate cash. The financing company then collects the payments from the customers who owe the money.

Revenue-based financing: This involves borrowing money from a lender in exchange for a percentage of the business's future revenue. This can be an attractive option for businesses that have consistent revenue streams but may not have a strong credit history.

Microloans: Microloans are small loans made to businesses or individuals. These loans are often used for small business expenses, such as purchasing equipment or inventory.

Advantages	Disadvantages
<ul><li>Access to capital outside of the traditional banking system</li><li>Can provide quick and easy access to capital</li><li>May be easier to qualify for than traditional bank loans</li><li>May have lower interest rates than traditional bank loans for borrowers with a weaker credit history</li></ul>	<ul><li>Interest rates may be higher than traditional bank loans for borrowers with a strong credit history</li><li>May require collateral or personal guarantees</li><li>Alternative financing companies may have stricter repayment terms or penalties for late payments</li><li>May not have the same regulatory oversight as traditional banks</li></ul>

CHAPTER 6

Financial Regulation

Financial regulation refers to a set of rules and guidelines created by government agencies or independent bodies to oversee and regulate financial institutions and markets. These regulations are designed to ensure the safety and stability of the financial system and protect consumers from fraud, abuse, and unfair practices.

Financial regulation is a critical component of modern economies, as it promotes transparency, stability, and fairness in the financial sector. This introductory guide aims to provide a comprehensive overview of financial regulation, including its history, key players, and important principles.

History of Financial Regulation Financial regulation has a long and complex history, dating back to ancient times. In medieval Europe, money lenders were regulated by guilds and city authorities, while in the United States, the first federal banking regulation was established in 1863 with the creation of the Office of the Comptroller of the Currency (OCC).

The Great Depression of the 1930s prompted significant changes in financial regulation, as governments sought to prevent future economic crises. The US government created the Securities and Exchange Commission (SEC) in 1934 to regulate the securities industry, while the Federal Deposit Insurance Corporation (FDIC) was established in 1933 to insure bank deposits and promote stability in the banking system.

In the wake of the 2008 financial crisis, global financial regulators, such as the Financial Stability Board (FSB) and the Basel Committee on Banking Supervision, have taken a more proactive approach to financial regulation, implementing a variety of new regulations to prevent another crisis.

Financial Regulatory Agencies

In order to enforce financial regulations, governments establish regulatory agencies with the responsibility of ensuring that financial institutions and markets operate within the legal framework. These agencies have a critical role in maintaining the stability of the financial system and protecting the interests of consumers and investors.

In this section, we will discuss the main regulatory agencies in the United States and their respective roles.

Securities and Exchange Commission (SEC)

The Securities and Exchange Commission (SEC) is the primary regulator of the securities markets in the United States. Its mission is to protect investors, maintain fair, orderly, and efficient markets, and facilitate capital formation. The SEC's responsibilities include the following:

- Registering securities and companies that issue them
- Regulating the disclosure of information about securities
- Enforcing laws and regulations governing the securities markets
- Monitoring the activities of brokers, dealers, and investment advisors
- Regulating the trading of securities on national exchanges
- Administering the laws governing mutual funds and other investment companies

Federal Reserve System (Fed)

The Federal Reserve System (Fed) is the central bank of the United States. Its primary responsibilities include conducting monetary policy, supervising and regulating banks, and maintaining the stability of the financial system. The Fed's regulatory functions include:

- Supervising and regulating banks, including the largest and most complex institutions.
- Conducting regular examinations of banks to ensure their safety and soundness
- Developing and enforcing rules and regulations for banks and other financial institutions
- Administering the laws that govern the operations of the financial system, including the Community Reinvestment Act and the Bank Secrecy Act
- Conducting research and analysis on financial markets and the economy

Commodity Futures Trading Commission (CFTC)

The Commodity Futures Trading Commission (CFTC) is the regulator of the futures and options markets in the United States. Its mission is to promote the integrity, resilience, and vibrancy of the U.S. derivatives markets through effective regulation. The CFTC's responsibilities include:

- Regulating the trading of futures and options contracts
- Ensuring that futures and options markets are fair, transparent, and competitive
- Registering and regulating commodity pool operators and commodity trading advisors
- Conducting investigations and enforcement actions to ensure compliance with the laws and regulations governing the derivatives markets

Federal Deposit Insurance Corporation (FDIC)

The Federal Deposit Insurance Corporation (FDIC) is an independent agency that provides deposit insurance to protect depositors in case of bank failures. The FDIC's primary responsibilities include:

- ❖ Insuring deposits in banks and savings associations up to certain limits
- ❖ Monitoring and addressing risks to the stability of the banking system
- ❖ Resolving failed banks and savings associations
- ❖ Promoting the safety and soundness of the banking system
- ❖ Regulating and supervising certain state-chartered banks that are not members of the Federal Reserve System

Office of the Comptroller of the Currency (OCC)

The Office of the Comptroller of the Currency (OCC) is an independent bureau of the U.S. Department of the Treasury that supervises and regulates national banks and federal savings associations. The OCC's responsibilities include:

- Ensuring the safety and soundness of national banks and federal savings associations
- Ensuring that these institutions operate in compliance with applicable laws and regulations
- Enforcing laws and regulations that govern the activities of national banks and federal savings associations
- Issuing and enforcing rules and regulations that govern the operations of national banks and federal savings associations

The National Credit Union Administration (NCUA) is an independent agency that regulates and supervises federally insured credit unions in the United States.

Consumer Financial Protection Bureau (CFPB)

The Consumer Financial Protection Bureau (CFPB) is an independent agency responsible for enforcing consumer financial protection laws and regulating financial products and services offered to consumers. The CFPB's responsibilities include:

- Protecting consumers from unfair, deceptive, or abusive practices in the financial industry
- Promoting financial education and literacy among consumers
- Enforcing laws and regulations governing the financial industry, including the Fair Credit Reporting Act, the Truth in Lending Act, and the Real Estate Settlement Procedures Act
- Regulating financial products and services offered to consumers, including mortgages, credit cards, and payday loans

Financial Industry Regulatory Authority (FINRA)

The Financial Industry Regulatory Authority (FINRA) is a private, non-profit organization that regulates the activities of broker-dealers in the United States. FINRA's responsibilities include:

- Registering and regulating broker-dealers that operate in the securities markets
- Administering the licensing exams that financial professionals must pass to become registered representatives
- Enforcing rules and regulations that govern the activities of broker-dealers and their registered representatives
- Monitoring and regulating the trading activities of broker-dealers

In addition to federal regulatory agencies, each state has its own regulatory agencies that oversee financial institutions and markets within the state. These agencies are responsible for enforcing state laws and regulations that govern the activities of financial institutions, including banks, credit unions, and insurance companies.

Types of Financial Regulations

Financial regulations are rules and guidelines that are put in place by government or regulatory agencies to oversee financial activities and promote stability and fairness in financial markets. Financial regulations can take various forms, and in this section, we will discuss the most common types of financial regulations.

Prudential regulation aims to promote the safety and soundness of financial institutions by setting requirements for capital, liquidity, and risk management. The goal of prudential regulation is to prevent financial institutions from taking on too much risk and to ensure that they have sufficient capital and liquidity to absorb losses in the event of a financial crisis.

Prudential regulations are often implemented by central banks, such as the Federal Reserve in the United States, and regulatory agencies that oversee financial institutions, such as the Office of the Comptroller of the Currency (OCC) and the Federal Deposit Insurance Corporation (FDIC).

Conduct regulation focuses on promoting fair and transparent practices in financial markets and preventing fraud, market manipulation, and other forms of misconduct. Conduct regulations are typically implemented by securities regulators, such as the Securities and Exchange Commission (SEC) in the United States, and market regulators, such as the Commodity Futures Trading Commission (CFTC).

Conduct regulations can take various forms, such as rules governing the disclosure of information to investors, restrictions on insider trading, and prohibitions on market manipulation.

Systemic risk regulation aims to prevent and mitigate risks that can lead to financial crises and widespread economic instability. Systemic risk regulations focus on identifying and addressing risks that can threaten the stability of the financial system, such as the interconnectedness of financial institutions, the use of complex financial instruments, and the concentration of risk in certain sectors.

Systemic risk regulations are often implemented by central banks and regulatory agencies that oversee the financial system, such as the Financial Stability Oversight Council (FSOC) in the United States.

Consumer protection regulation aims to protect consumers from abusive and fraudulent practices in the financial industry. Consumer protection regulations cover a wide range of financial products and services, including mortgages, credit cards, auto loans, and insurance.

Consumer protection regulations are typically implemented by regulatory agencies that specialize in consumer protection, such as the Consumer Financial Protection Bureau (CFPB) in the United States.

Market entry regulation refers to rules and requirements that financial firms must meet to enter and operate in financial markets. Market entry regulations can include licensing requirements, minimum capital requirements, and other regulatory barriers to entry.

Market entry regulations are often implemented by regulatory agencies that oversee financial institutions and markets, such as the Securities and Exchange Commission (SEC) and the Commodity Futures Trading Commission (CFTC).

Financial regulations serve many important purposes and provide several benefits to both the financial system and the broader economy. In this section, we will discuss some of the key benefits of financial regulations.

One of the primary benefits of financial regulations is that they promote financial stability by reducing the likelihood and severity of financial crises. Regulations can help prevent institutions from taking on excessive risk, which can destabilize the financial system and lead to widespread economic impacts. By setting standards for risk management, capital requirements, and other measures, financial regulations can help ensure that financial institutions are better prepared to weather economic shocks and crises.

Financial regulations also provide important protections for consumers and investors. Regulations can require financial institutions to be transparent about their fees, terms, and conditions, and to provide accurate and timely information to consumers and investors. Regulations can also prevent financial institutions from engaging in predatory or fraudulent practices that can harm consumers and investors. By ensuring that financial institutions are operating in a fair and transparent manner, financial regulations can help consumers and investors make more informed decisions and protect themselves from financial harm.

While financial regulations are often seen as constraints on the financial industry, they can also foster competition and innovation. Regulations can help level the playing field for smaller or newer players in the financial industry, by setting standards that apply equally to all firms. Regulations can also encourage the development of new financial products and services that are safer and more innovative, by providing clear guidelines for what is acceptable and what is not.

Financial regulations can also play a role in promoting economic growth. Regulations can help ensure that financial institutions are operating in a safe and stable manner, which can increase confidence in the financial system and promote investment. By reducing the risk of financial crises, regulations can also reduce the negative economic impacts of such crises, such as job losses and reduced economic activity. Additionally, regulations can promote financial inclusion and consumer protection, which can help more people participate in the financial system and contribute to economic growth.

CHAPTER 7

Financial Ratios

Financial ratios are tools that businesses use to check how well they're doing financially, see if they're making money, and figure out if they can pay their bills. These ratios come from important financial reports like the balance sheet, income statement, and cash flow statement. Investors and lenders look at these ratios to see if the business is healthy and has the potential to grow.

There are different kinds of financial ratios that tell us various things about a business's financial health. These include liquidity ratios, profitability ratios, activity ratios, and debt ratios. Each type of ratio helps people understand different aspects of the business's finances.

Liquidity ratios are especially important because they show whether a business can quickly turn its assets into cash to pay off its debts. This is crucial for anyone who wants to know if the business can handle its short-term obligations. The most common liquidity ratios are the current ratio and the quick ratio, which help assess the company's ability to manage and pay off its immediate debts.

Current Ratio

The current ratio is a financial metric that assesses a company's ability to cover its short-term debts with its short-term assets. It compares what the company owns that can be turned into cash within a year—like cash itself, money owed by customers, stock on hand, and prepayments—to what it owes in the coming year, including bills, short-term loans, and the due portion of longer-term debts.

Here's how to calculate the current ratio:

$$\text{Current Ratio} = \frac{\text{Current Assets}}{\text{Current Liabilities}}$$

For instance, if a company has $100,000 in current assets and $50,000 in current liabilities, the current ratio would be:

$$\text{Current Ratio} = \frac{\$100,000}{\$50,000} = 2$$

A current ratio of 2 indicates that the company has twice as much in easily accessible assets as it has in debts due within the year, suggesting it's well-prepared to meet its short-term financial responsibilities.

However, a very high current ratio could suggest that a company has more cash or inventory than it might need, which might not always be positive. It could imply that the company isn't using its assets effectively to grow. In such scenarios, the quick ratio might be a better indicator of liquidity as it excludes inventory from assets and provides a more conservative view of a company's financial health.

Quick Ratio

The quick ratio, often referred to as the acid-test ratio, offers a stringent evaluation of a company's immediate liquidity by focusing on assets that can be swiftly converted into cash. This calculation leaves out inventory, as it's not always quick to sell.

Here's the formula to calculate the quick ratio:

$$\text{Quick Ratio} = \frac{(\text{Current Assets} - \text{Inventory})}{\text{Current Liabilities}}$$

For instance, if a company has current assets totaling $100,000, with $30,000 tied up in inventory, and current liabilities of $50,000, the quick ratio would be calculated as follows:

$$\text{Quick Ratio} = \frac{(\$100,000 - \$30,000)}{\$50,000} = 1.4$$

A quick ratio of 1.4 suggests that the company has $1.40 in easily liquidated assets for every dollar of short-term liabilities, which is a good indicator of the company's capability to cover its immediate debts.

While liquidity ratios like the quick ratio are vital for understanding a company's capacity to handle short-term financial commitments, they don't shed light on the long-term financial health or profitability of the business. To gain a comprehensive view of a company's financial condition, it's crucial to analyze these figures alongside other financial ratios, such as profitability and solvency ratios. This broader approach helps paint a more complete picture of a company's overall financial performance.

Solvency Ratios

Solvency ratios are financial ratios that measure a company's ability to meet its long-term financial obligations. These ratios are used to assess a company's ability to pay its debts in the long run and its financial stability. Solvency ratios are important for investors, creditors, and management as they indicate a company's ability to continue operating and its financial health.

There are several types of solvency ratios, including debt-to-equity ratio, debt-to-asset ratio, interest coverage ratio, and fixed charge coverage ratio.

Debt-to-Equity Ratio

The debt-to-equity ratio is a financial metric that shows the balance between the amount of capital a company secures through debt and the amount obtained through shareholders' equity. Essentially, it reflects a company's ability to cover all of its outstanding debts should it need to settle them using its shareholders' funds.

To calculate the debt-to-equity ratio, you can use the following formula:

$$\text{Debt-to-Equity Ratio} = \frac{\text{Total Liabilities}}{\text{Shareholders' Equity}}$$

For instance, if a company has total liabilities of $500,000 and shareholders' equity of $1,000,000, the calculation of the debt-to-equity ratio would be:

$$\text{Debt-to-Equity Ratio} = \frac{\$500,000}{\$1,000,000} = 0.5$$

A debt-to-equity ratio of 0.5 indicates that for every dollar of equity, the company uses fifty cents of debt. This suggests that the company utilizes a moderate level of debt in its financing strategy, maintaining a balance that does not overly rely on borrowed funds. This can be seen as a positive sign, indicating that the company has managed to keep its borrowing at a manageable level relative to its equity.

Debt-to-Asset Ratio

The debt-to-asset ratio is a key financial metric that shows what portion of a company's assets is financed through debt. This ratio is crucial for understanding the level of financial risk a company carries and how much of its assets could potentially be claimed by creditors in case of financial distress.

To calculate the debt-to-asset ratio, use the formula:

$$\text{Debt-to-Asset Ratio} = \frac{\text{Total Liabilities}}{\text{Total Assets}}$$

For instance, consider a company with total liabilities of $500,000 and total assets of $1,500,000. The debt-to-asset ratio would be calculated as follows:

$$\text{Debt-to-Asset Ratio} = \frac{\$500,000}{\$1,500,000} = 0.33$$

A debt-to-asset ratio of 0.33 indicates that 33% of the company's assets are financed by debt. This relatively lower ratio suggests a conservative level of financial risk, with the majority of assets being financed through means other than debt. This can be seen as a favorable indicator of financial stability, showing that the company is not overly reliant on borrowing to fund its operations.

Interest Coverage Ratio

The interest coverage ratio is a financial metric used to determine a company's ability to handle its debt obligations by comparing its earnings before interest and taxes (EBIT) to its interest expenses. This ratio is crucial because it shows how many times a company can pay off its interest expenses with its current earnings, which is a key indicator of financial health.

To calculate the interest coverage ratio, you can use the following formula:

$$\text{Interest Coverage Ratio} = \frac{\text{EBIT}}{\text{Interest Expenses}}$$

For example, consider a company that has an EBIT of $200,000 and faces interest expenses of $50,000. The calculation of the interest coverage ratio would be:

$$\text{Interest Coverage Ratio} = \frac{\$200,000}{\$50,000} = 4$$

An interest coverage ratio of 4 implies that the company earns enough to cover its interest expenses four times over. This suggests that the company is in a strong financial position when it comes to meeting its debt obligations, as it generates significantly more in earnings than it needs to spend on interest.

Fixed Charge Coverage Ratio

The fixed charge coverage ratio is an important financial metric that extends beyond the interest coverage ratio by considering not only interest expenses but also lease payments and other fixed obligations. This ratio provides a broader view of a company's ability to meet its fixed financial commitments using its earnings before interest, taxes, depreciation, and amortization (EBITDA).

To calculate the fixed charge coverage ratio, use the following formula:

$$\text{Fixed Charge Coverage Ratio} = \frac{\text{EBITDA}}{(\text{Interest Expenses} + \text{Lease Payments} + \text{Other Fixed Charges})}$$

For instance, let's say a company has an EBITDA of $300,000, interest expenses of $50,000, lease payments of $20,000, and other fixed charges amounting to $10,000. The calculation of the fixed charge coverage ratio would be:

$$\text{Fixed Charge Coverage Ratio} = \frac{\$300,000}{(\$50,000 + \$20,000 + \$10,000)} = \frac{\$300,000}{\$80,000} = 3.75$$

A fixed charge coverage ratio of 3.75 means that the company can cover its total fixed charges 3.75 times with its EBITDA, indicating a solid capability to meet these obligations. This high ratio suggests that the company generates substantially more earnings than needed to cover its fixed charges, positioning it well to handle financial commitments and potential economic fluctuations.

Profitability Ratios

Profitability ratios are a set of financial ratios that help to evaluate a company's ability to generate profits from its operations. Profitability ratios are useful for investors and business owners who want to understand how well a company is performing in terms of generating profits. The three main profitability ratios are gross profit margin, net profit margin, and return on investment.

Gross Profit Margin

The gross profit margin is a profitability ratio that measures the amount of money a company makes on its sales after subtracting the cost of goods sold (COGS). It is expressed as a percentage and calculated by dividing the gross profit by the revenue.

$$Gross\ profit\ margin = (Revenue - COGS)/Revenue$$

The gross profit margin helps to evaluate a company's ability to generate profits from its products or services. A higher gross profit margin indicates that the company is earning more on its sales and has a better ability to cover its operating expenses.

Net Profit Margin

The net profit margin is a profitability ratio that measures the amount of profit a company makes after subtracting all its expenses, including operating expenses, interest, taxes, and other expenses. It is expressed as a percentage and calculated by dividing the net profit by the revenue.

$$Net\ profit\ margin = (Net\ profit/Revenue) \times 100$$

The net profit margin helps to evaluate a company's ability to generate profits after all expenses have been paid. A higher net profit margin indicates that the company has better control over its expenses and a better ability to generate profits.

Return on Investment (ROI)

The return on investment (ROI) is a profitability ratio that measures the return on investment made in a company. It is expressed as a percentage and calculated by dividing the net profit by the total assets.

$$ROI = (Net\ profit/Total\ assets) \times 100$$

The ROI helps to evaluate a company's ability to generate profits from its assets. A higher ROI indicates that the company is generating more profit from its assets and has a better ability to grow its business.

Efficiency Ratios

Efficiency ratios are a set of financial ratios that help to evaluate a company's ability to use its assets and liabilities to generate sales and profits. Efficiency ratios are useful for investors and business owners who want to understand how well a company is managing its resources to generate profits. The three main efficiency ratios are asset turnover, inventory turnover, and accounts receivable turnover.

Asset Turnover

The asset turnover ratio is an efficiency ratio that measures the amount of revenue a company generates per dollar of assets it owns. It is expressed as a ratio and calculated by dividing the revenue by the total assets.

$$Asset\ Turnover = Revenue\ /\ Total\ Assets$$

The asset turnover ratio helps to evaluate a company's ability to generate revenue from its assets. A higher asset turnover ratio indicates that the company is generating more revenue from its assets and has a better ability to manage its assets effectively.

Inventory Turnover

The inventory turnover ratio is an efficiency ratio that measures the number of times a company sells and replaces its inventory during a period. It is expressed as a ratio and calculated by dividing the cost of goods sold by the average inventory.

$$Inventory\ Turnover = Cost\ of\ Goods\ Sold\ /\ Average\ Inventory$$

The inventory turnover ratio helps to evaluate a company's ability to manage its inventory. A higher inventory turnover ratio indicates that the company is selling its inventory more quickly and has a better ability to manage its inventory effectively.

Accounts Receivable Turnover

The accounts receivable turnover ratio is an efficiency ratio that measures the number of times a company collects its accounts receivable during a period. It is expressed as a ratio and calculated by dividing the revenue by the average accounts receivable.

$$Accounts\ Receivable\ Turnover = Revenue\ /\ Average\ Accounts\ Receivable$$

The accounts receivable turnover ratio helps to evaluate a company's ability to manage its accounts receivable. A higher accounts receivable turnover ratio indicates that the company is collecting its accounts receivable more quickly and has a better ability to manage its cash flow.

Payables Turnover

The payables turnover ratio is an efficiency ratio that measures how quickly a company pays its bills. It is expressed as a ratio and calculated by dividing the cost of goods sold by the average accounts payable.

Payables Turnover = Cost of Goods Sold / Average Accounts Payable

The payables turnover ratio helps to evaluate a company's ability to manage its payables. A higher payables turnover ratio indicates that the company is paying its bills more quickly and has a better ability to manage its cash flow.

Working Capital Turnover

The working capital turnover ratio is an efficiency ratio that measures the amount of revenue generated per dollar of working capital. It is expressed as a ratio and calculated by dividing the revenue by the working capital.

Working Capital Turnover = Revenue / Working Capital

The working capital turnover ratio helps to evaluate a company's ability to generate revenue with the working capital it has. A higher working capital turnover ratio indicates that the company is generating more revenue with its working capital and has a better ability to manage its resources effectively.

Efficiency ratios are useful tools that help investors and business owners understand how well a company uses its assets and liabilities to make sales and profits. For example, the asset turnover ratio indicates how effectively the company generates revenue from its assets. The inventory turnover ratio shows how well the company manages its stock. The accounts receivable turnover ratio reveals how quickly the company collects money owed by its customers, while the payables turnover ratio assesses how the company handles its obligations to suppliers. Lastly, the working capital turnover ratio measures how efficiently the company uses its available capital to generate sales. Understanding these ratios allows investors and business owners to make smarter decisions about investing in or managing the company, providing insights into the company's operational efficiency and financial health.

CHAPTER 8

Financial Markets

Financial markets play a critical role in the global economy, providing a platform for the exchange of financial assets, such as stocks, bonds, and commodities, between buyers and sellers. Financial markets allow businesses and individuals to raise capital, manage risk, and invest in a variety of assets. In this article, we will provide an introduction to financial markets, including the types of financial markets, the participants in financial markets, and the key factors that influence financial markets.

Types of Financial Markets

There are various types of financial market.

Capital Markets

Capital markets are venues where financial products like stocks, bonds, and real estate are traded, and they primarily serve to raise long-term investments for businesses and governments. These markets allow companies and governments to sell securities to the public to fund their operations. Capital markets are split into primary and secondary markets.

In the primary market, new securities are issued by companies and governments to gather funds from investors. This could include stocks, bonds, or other financial instruments. It's a crucial funding source for issuers and offers investors the opportunity to buy securities at their initial prices.

The secondary market, on the other hand, is where these existing securities are traded between investors. This trading happens at market prices and provides liquidity to the primary market, enabling investors to offload their holdings and withdraw their investments. Stock exchanges are typical examples of secondary markets.

Money markets focus on short-term debt securities, like Treasury bills, commercial paper, and certificates of deposit, providing short-term liquidity for businesses and governments. These markets are essential for financing day-to-day operations and are characterized by high liquidity and low risk. Returns on money market investments are usually lower compared to other financial markets, but they offer stability and low volatility, making them a safe option for investors during periods of market turbulence.

Foreign Exchange Markets

Foreign exchange markets, also known as Forex or FX markets, are the financial markets that deal with the trading of currencies. The primary function of foreign exchange markets is to facilitate international trade and investment. Foreign exchange markets provide a platform for businesses and individuals to exchange one currency for another.

Foreign exchange markets are the largest financial markets in the world, with daily trading volumes exceeding $5 trillion. These markets operate 24 hours a day, 5 days a week, and are accessible to investors all over the world. The most commonly traded currencies in foreign exchange markets are the US dollar, Euro, Japanese yen, British pound, and Swiss franc.

Derivatives Markets

Derivatives markets are the financial markets that deal with financial instruments whose value is derived from an underlying asset, such as stocks, bonds, currencies, or commodities. Derivatives markets are used for risk management, speculation, and hedging. The primary function of derivatives markets is to provide a platform for investors to manage their risks and exposure to financial assets.

Derivatives markets are divided into two types: exchange-traded derivatives and over-the-counter (OTC) derivatives. Exchange-traded derivatives are traded on a regulated exchange, while OTC derivatives are traded between two parties directly.

Commodity Markets

Commodity markets are the financial markets that deal with the trading of physical commodities, such as gold, silver, crude oil, and agricultural products. The primary function of commodity markets is to provide a platform for producers, consumers, and investors to buy and sell commodities.

Commodity markets are usually highly volatile than other financial markets because the price of commodities is affected by a range of factors, such as global supply and demand, geopolitical events, and weather conditions. Commodity markets are divided into two types: spot markets and futures markets.

Spot markets are the physical markets where commodities are traded for immediate delivery. In the spot market, the price of the commodity is determined by supply and demand. Spot markets provide a platform for producers and consumers to buy and sell commodities at current market prices.

Futures markets are the financial markets where commodities are traded for future delivery. In the futures market, investors can buy or sell contracts that specify the delivery of a certain amount of a commodity at a future date. Futures markets provide a platform for investors to hedge their exposure to price fluctuations in the commodities market.

Interbank Markets

Interbank markets are the financial markets where banks and other financial institutions lend and borrow money from each other. The primary function of interbank markets is to provide short-term liquidity to banks and other financial institutions.

Interbank markets are important for the smooth functioning of the banking system. Banks use interbank markets to manage their cash flows and meet their reserve requirements. Interbank markets are usually highly regulated and operate under strict guidelines set by central banks.

Mortgage Markets

Mortgage markets are the financial markets where home mortgages are originated, sold, and securitized. The primary function of mortgage markets is to provide a platform for individuals and businesses to finance their real estate investments.

Mortgage markets are divided into two types: primary mortgage markets and secondary mortgage markets. In the primary mortgage market, lenders originate and issue mortgages to borrowers. In the secondary mortgage market, mortgages are sold and securitized into mortgage-backed securities, which are then sold to investors.

Mortgage markets are important for the economy as they facilitate home ownership and real estate investment. Mortgage markets also play a crucial role in the global financial system, as the collapse of the US mortgage market was one of the primary causes of the global financial crisis in 2008.

Role of Financial Markets

Financial markets play a critical role in the global economy by facilitating the flow of capital between savers and investors, enabling businesses to raise capital, and providing a platform for individuals and institutions to manage risk and invest in financial assets. In this article, we will explore the role of financial markets in more detail, examining their functions, types, and key players.

Functions of Financial Markets

Financial markets play an essential role in shaping the economy by allowing businesses to access capital that fuels their growth and innovation. When companies issue stocks, they not only share ownership but also potential profits with investors. Similarly, bonds are promises to repay borrowed funds with interest, offering a steady income to bondholders.

These markets ensure that assets can be quickly and easily traded, providing the liquidity that investors need. This liquidity makes securities more attractive, boosting confidence among investors and allowing them to buy or sell assets without significantly affecting their prices.

Risk management is another critical function of financial markets. They offer a variety of financial instruments, such as futures and options, which investors use to protect themselves against potential losses due to fluctuations in interest rates, currency values, and commodity prices. This hedging ability is crucial for maintaining financial stability.

Financial markets serve as a venue where the prices of financial assets are established. These prices result from the continuous interaction between buyers and sellers, influenced by various factors including economic indicators, company performance, geopolitical developments, and overall market sentiment. This price discovery process is vital as it reflects the collective assessment of all market participants, providing valuable information that helps investors make informed decisions.

Financial markets are indispensable to the economic system. They not only help in raising capital and providing liquidity but also play significant roles in risk management and price determination, contributing to economic growth and stability. This dynamic environment requires businesses and investors to remain well-informed and responsive to market conditions.

Financial Market Participants

Financial markets are crucial because they help businesses get the money they need to grow and develop new products. When a company sells stocks, it's inviting investors to own a part of the company and potentially share in its profits. On the other hand, when a company issues bonds, it's borrowing money from investors with a promise to pay back that money with interest.

These markets also make it easy for people to buy and sell assets like stocks and bonds quickly. This is known as liquidity and is important because it lets investors move their money around without too much trouble or loss in value. It helps keep the market moving smoothly and builds confidence among investors.

Another important role of financial markets is helping companies and investors manage risk. They provide tools like futures and options—kinds of contracts that allow people to set prices now for buying or selling something later on. These tools help protect against prices going up or down unexpectedly.

Financial markets also help set the prices for these assets through what's called price discovery. This happens as buyers and sellers make deals, and it helps everyone understand what a fair price might look like based on current market conditions

Function	Explanation
Raising Capital	Businesses can secure funding for expansion by selling stocks or bonds.
Providing Liquidity	Ensures easy trading of securities, enabling quick access to funds.
Risk Management	Includes financial instruments like futures and options for controlling financial risks.
Price Discovery	Facilitates the determination of asset values through active trading.

CHAPTER 9

International Finance

International finance is a field that deals with financial transactions and interactions between different countries. It is a complex area that encompasses various topics like exchange rates, international trade, foreign investments, and global financial markets. International finance is crucial for businesses and governments operating in a globalized world as it provides them with the necessary tools to manage and navigate complex financial situations.

International finance is a subset of the broader field of finance, which is concerned with the management of money and other assets. However, it differs from domestic finance in that it involves dealing with different currencies, legal systems, and economic policies. International finance is essential for companies that operate in different countries, as they need to manage their financial resources in various currencies and in different legal and regulatory environments.

One of the critical aspects of international finance is the exchange rate, which refers to the value of one currency in relation to another. Exchange rates are determined by supply and demand factors in the global foreign exchange market. The exchange rate affects the competitiveness of a country's exports and imports, as well as the cost of borrowing and lending money. Exchange rates are also affected by economic factors such as inflation, interest rates, and government policies.

Another important aspect of international finance is international trade, which involves the exchange of goods and services between different countries. International trade is driven by comparative advantages, which refers to a country's ability to produce a particular product or service more efficiently than another country. International trade is essential for economic growth as it allows countries to specialize in the production of goods and services in which they have a comparative advantage and to import goods and services that are produced more efficiently in other countries.

Foreign investments are another key component of international finance. Foreign investments refer to the acquisition of assets or ownership stakes in companies located in foreign countries. Foreign investments can take various forms, such as direct investments, portfolio investments, and foreign loans. Foreign investments can be attractive for companies as they provide access to new markets and resources, and they can also diversify risks.

Global financial markets are also an essential aspect of international finance. Financial markets provide a platform for the buying and selling of financial assets, such as stocks, bonds, currencies, and commodities. Global financial markets are interconnected, and movements in one market can have significant impacts on other markets. Financial markets are subject to various risks, such as market risk, credit risk, and liquidity risk.

The management of international finance is complex, and it requires specialized skills and knowledge. International finance professionals need to be able to analyze economic and financial data from different countries, understand the risks associated with different financial instruments, and develop strategies to manage those risks. International finance professionals also need to be familiar with international legal and regulatory frameworks and be able to navigate different cultural and language barriers.

International finance is a critical field that is essential for businesses and governments operating in a globalized world. It involves various aspects such as exchange rates, international trade, foreign investments, and global financial markets. The management of international finance is complex and requires specialized skills and knowledge. The field of international finance is constantly evolving, and new challenges and opportunities continue to arise, making it an exciting and dynamic field.

Foreign Exchange Market

The foreign exchange market, or forex market, is a vast, decentralized marketplace for trading currencies. It's the largest financial market globally, with over $6 trillion traded daily. This market is essential for international trade and investment, enabling businesses and investors to buy, sell, and exchange currencies.

Trading in the forex market occurs directly between parties in an over-the-counter (OTC) manner through a network of banks, brokers, and dealers. This allows for trading around the clock during weekdays, accommodating global time zones.

Currencies in the forex market are traded in pairs, like EUR/USD or USD/JPY. The exchange rate between these pairs is driven by supply and demand, influenced by factors like economic stability, political events, and monetary policy from central bank

Feature	Explanation
Market Nature	Global, decentralized, OTC
Trading Hours	24 hours a day, five days a week
Currency Trading	Pairs, driven by supply and demand
Key Influences	Economic data, political events, central bank policies
Participants	Banks, corporations, hedge funds, individual traders
Regulation	Bodies like CFTC (US), FCA (UK), ASIC (Australia) oversee activities

The market involves various participants including banks which are the largest traders, corporations that need to hedge exposure to currency risk, hedge funds that try to profit from currency fluctuations, and individual traders who use online platforms and brokers.

Although the forex market offers significant opportunities, it also comes with risks. It's important for traders to understand the market mechanisms and the factors affecting currency values before engaging in trading.

International Trade Finance

International trade finance comprises the financial tools and services that support the buying and selling of goods and services across borders, playing a crucial role in global economic growth and development. The process can be complex and carries significant risks, which these financial instruments help mitigate, ensuring secure and efficient transactions.

Key players in international trade finance include importers who buy goods from overseas, exporters who sell abroad, banks, and financial institutions that offer various services to facilitate these exchanges. These services include issuing letters of credit, providing trade finance, and offering foreign exchange solutions.

A letter of credit is especially vital in international trade finance. It acts as a guarantee from a bank that payment will be made to the exporter, provided that the terms specified in the letter are met. This tool not only secures payment for the exporter but also minimizes the non-payment risk for the importer and can help resolve disputes.

Different types of letters of credit include commercial, standby, revocable, and irrevocable. Each serves different purposes, such as facilitating transactions or providing a guarantee.

Trade finance is another critical element, offering financing solutions that support the trade cycle. This might be pre-shipment finance that provides the exporter with working capital before shipping goods or post-shipment finance that occurs after the goods have been sent.

Foreign exchange services are essential in managing currency exchanges necessary for international trade. Offered by banks and currency brokers, these services help businesses manage currency risks associated with transactions in foreign currencies.

Moreover, international trade finance must adhere to various international regulations and standards, like those set by the World Trade Organization (WTO) and the International Chamber of Commerce (ICC). Compliance ensures a fair and transparent trading environment.

Despite its benefits, international trade finance also presents challenges, including credit, foreign exchange, and political risks. Businesses can manage these risks through financial instruments like letters of credit and by engaging in hedging strategies.

Financial Instrument	Function
Letters of Credit	Guarantees payment to exporters under set terms.
Trade Finance	Provides funding to support the trade cycle.
Foreign Exchange Services	Manages currency transactions and risks.

International trade finance not only facilitates transactions but also provides liquidity, reduces trading risks, and enhances efficiency in the global marketplace. Despite facing challenges like access to finance and navigating a complex and fragmented system, its role in promoting economic growth and supporting international trade remains indispensable. As globalization increases and cross-border trade grows, the significance of trade finance continues to rise, making it a key area for continual development and innovation.

International Investment

International investment involves putting money into assets and companies located outside one's home country. This can include stocks, bonds, real estate, and various other financial instruments. The goal of international investment is to diversify an investment portfolio and possibly achieve higher returns by capitalizing on opportunities in foreign markets.

Investors can engage in different forms of international investment. Foreign direct investment (FDI) occurs when a company invests directly in facilities or operations in another country, taking a hands-on approach to its investment. Foreign portfolio investment (FPI) entails investing in securities such as stocks or bonds of companies located in other countries, usually without direct control over the businesses. Additionally, international venture capital focuses on providing funding to startups and early-stage companies abroad, often bringing not just capital but also strategic support to these burgeoning enterprises.

There are significant benefits to international investment. It allows investors to diversify their holdings across global markets, potentially reducing risk and tapping into faster-growing economies. It also enables them to benefit from variations in currencies and interest rates, which can provide a hedge against inflation and economic fluctuations in their home country.

Moreover, international investments can drive growth and expansion for companies. By entering foreign markets, companies can access new customer bases and leverage lower labor costs or favorable tax policies offered by host countries.

However, these opportunities come with their share of risks and challenges. Currency risk is a major concern, as fluctuations in exchange rates can significantly affect the return on investment. Investors often need to use hedging strategies to manage this risk. Political and economic instability in the investment country can also affect the value and security of international investments. Moreover, cultural and language differences can complicate the management and operation of foreign investments, requiring local partnerships or specialized staff to navigate these challenges effectively.

Despite these risks, international investment is a critical component of the global economy, increasingly vital as globalization progresses. It offers significant opportunities for growth and development, both for investors and the economies of the investment destinations.

Here's how international investment can be approached:

- **Direct Investment**: Companies might set up new operations or acquire businesses abroad, gaining significant control and local market insights but also facing higher complexity and costs.
- **Portfolio Investment**: Investors buy foreign stocks or bonds, often through mutual funds or ETFs, gaining exposure to international markets without direct management responsibilities, though this can be riskier.
- **Venture Capital**: Providing capital to overseas startups, offering crucial growth funding but with higher risks due to the inherent instability of early-stage companies.

Navigating the regulatory landscape of international investment, which varies widely by country, is essential for success. Regulations might be geared toward promoting domestic investment or protecting national interests, adding layers of complexity to international investment strategies.

As the world becomes more interconnected, the importance of effectively managing international investments continues to grow. Those who can skillfully handle the challenges and leverage the opportunities are well-positioned to achieve substantial returns and contribute to global economic development.

Type of Investment	Control Level	Market Exposure	Typical Investors
Foreign Direct Investment (FDI)	High	Direct involvement in foreign markets	Large corporations
Foreign Portfolio Investment (FPI)	Low	Indirect exposure through securities	Individual investors, mutual funds
International Venture Capital	Medium	Direct involvement, high risk	Venture capitalists

CHAPTER 10

Stock Market

The stock market, also known as the equity market, is a market where publicly traded companies issue and trade their stocks or shares. It is a platform for investors to buy and sell shares of a company, and it helps companies raise capital to fund their growth and expansion plans. The stock market is a critical component of the global financial system, and it plays a vital role in facilitating investment, economic growth, and development.

The stock market offers a platform for companies to raise funds for their operations by issuing shares to investors. Companies issue two types of stocks: common stocks and preferred stocks. Common stocks represent ownership in a company and give investors the right to vote in shareholder meetings and receive dividends, if the company declares them. Preferred stocks, on the other hand, do not provide voting rights, but they guarantee a fixed dividend payment to investors.

The stock market operates through stock exchanges, which are platforms where buyers and sellers meet to trade shares of publicly traded companies. In the United States, the two major stock exchanges are the New York Stock Exchange (NYSE) and the NASDAQ. The NYSE is the oldest and largest stock exchange in the world, while the NASDAQ is known for its technology-focused stocks.

The stock market also has many other players, including brokers, traders, market makers, and regulators. Brokers are intermediaries who facilitate the buying and selling of stocks by connecting buyers and sellers. Traders are individuals or institutions who buy and sell stocks in the market for profit. Market makers are financial firms that buy and sell stocks to ensure liquidity in the market. Regulators oversee the functioning of the stock market and ensure that market participants comply with the relevant laws and regulations.

The stock market can be both a source of opportunity and a source of risk for investors. On the one hand, investing in the stock market provides an opportunity for individuals to grow their wealth by participating in the growth of successful companies. On the other hand, investing in the stock market can be risky, as it is subject to the volatility of the market, economic conditions, and other factors.

To navigate the stock market successfully, investors need to have a solid understanding of the market's mechanics and the risks involved. They also need to conduct thorough research on the companies they plan to invest in, including their financial statements, management team, and growth prospects. Additionally, investors need to diversify their investments across multiple companies and sectors to minimize their risk.

The stock market is a critical component of the global financial system and provides a platform for companies to raise capital and for investors to buy and sell shares. Understanding the workings of the stock market and the risks involved is essential for investors who want to participate in the market and grow their wealth over time.

Types of Stock

The stock market is a complex and constantly changing entity where the prices of stocks are influenced by a multitude of factors. From macroeconomic indicators to company-specific events, various elements come together to determine how a stock is priced at any given moment. Here's a deeper look at these mechanisms and influences.

At its core, stock price determination hinges on the principles of supply and demand. If more investors want to buy a stock than sell it, the price will likely rise. Conversely, if more want to sell than buy, the price tends to drop. This balance is influenced not just by investor perception but also by concrete factors such as the company's financial performance, broader economic conditions, and market sentiment.

Financial performance is a critical driver in valuing a stock. Indicators such as earnings, revenue growth, profit margins, and projections of future performance play a significant role in attracting investors. Companies that show strong financial health tend to see their stock prices rise, whereas those with disappointing results might see declines.

The broader economic landscape also affects stock prices significantly. Indicators like GDP growth, unemployment rates, interest rates, and inflation can alter investor expectations about the market's future direction. For example, high interest rates can reduce consumer spending and increase borrowing costs, which may lower stock prices.

Investor sentiment can dramatically sway stock prices. This sentiment can be influenced by media, news, and market speculations. Positive sentiment can lead to price increases, while negative sentiment can drive prices down, demonstrating how psychological factors play into trading dynamics.

Additionally, news and global events are pivotal in shaping stock prices. Political instability, economic policy changes, international conflicts, or significant corporate announcements can lead to market volatility. For instance, a company announcing groundbreaking technology might see its stock price soar, while one involved in a scandal might see its value plummet.

Industry-specific developments also play a role. Changes in regulatory environments, technological advancements, or shifts in consumer preferences can impact companies differently based on their industry. For example, regulatory changes in the healthcare sector can affect pharmaceutical companies in significant ways.

Many investors also rely on technical analysis, which uses past market data to predict future price movements. By examining patterns in price actions and volume, investors attempt to anticipate what might happen next, influencing their buying and selling decisions.

Despite the potential for substantial returns, investing in stocks comes with various risks. These include market risk, where the value of investments can decline due to economic developments that impact the entire market; liquidity risk, which is the risk of not being able to sell stocks quickly enough; and currency risk, which comes into play with international investments as exchange rate fluctuations can affect profitability.

Investors use several strategies to manage these risks. Diversification across various financial instruments and industries can help mitigate the risk of significant losses. Hedging, using financial instruments like options and futures, can protect against downsides. Additionally, fundamental analysis of a company's financial health and industry position can aid in making informed investment decisions.

In summary, the stock market's nature requires a keen understanding of both the financial and psychological factors that drive it. By considering everything from economic conditions to individual company performance and global events, investors can navigate this volatile landscape. Effective risk management and a robust understanding of market dynamics are

Table of Key Influences on Stock Prices

Influencing Factor	Impact on Stock Prices
Supply and Demand	Direct impact through balance of buying and selling pressures.
Company Financial Performance	Earnings and growth prospects can attract or repel investors.
Economic Conditions	Macro indicators like GDP and interest rates shape investor expectations and risk assessments.

Influencing Factor	Impact on Stock Prices
Investor Sentiment	Psychological factor; positive sentiment can inflate prices, negative can deflate.
News and Global Events	Can trigger sudden and significant price changes based on market perception and reaction to the event.
Industry Trends	Sector-specific changes can affect related company stocks differently depending on the nature of the news.
Technical Analysis	Used to predict future movements based on historical data; affects trading decisions.
Market Risks	Includes market, liquidity, and currency risks which require management strategies to mitigate potential losses.

Stock Market Indices

Stock market indices are fundamental tools in the realm of finance, offering critical insights into the performance of groups of stocks that represent specific markets or sectors within them. These indices serve as benchmarks against which investors measure the overall health of a market, track trends, and make informed investment decisions.

At its essence, a stock market index is a statistical measure that tracks the performance of a basket of stocks. This basket is carefully selected to represent a particular market, sector, or investment strategy. Indices provide a snapshot of how stocks within the index are performing collectively over time, reflecting changes in market sentiment, economic conditions, and sector-specific dynamics.

There are several types of stock market indices

Broad-Based Indices: These indices aim to capture the overall performance of a market. For instance, the S&P 500 in the United States comprises 500 large-cap companies, representing a significant portion of the U.S. stock market. Broad-based indices are often used as benchmarks for assessing the general market direction and economic health.

Sector Indices: Sector-specific indices focus on industries such as technology, healthcare, energy, or financials. These indices allow investors to track the performance of specific sectors within the economy, providing insights into sector trends and opportunities. For example, the

Technology Select Sector SPDR Fund (XLK) tracks the performance of technology stocks within the S&P 500.

International Indices: International indices measure the performance of stocks outside an investor's home country. They offer exposure to global markets and enable diversification across different regions and economies. The MSCI EAFE Index covers developed markets in Europe, Australia, and the Far East, while the MSCI Emerging Markets Index tracks stocks in emerging economies worldwide.

Specialty Indices: These indices cater to specific investment styles or strategies, such as small-cap stocks, value stocks, or growth stocks. Specialty indices allow investors to focus on particular market segments that align with their investment objectives. The iShares Russell 2000 ETF (IWM), for example, tracks small-cap stocks in the U.S., offering exposure to smaller, potentially higher-growth companies.

Stock market indices are calculated using different methodologies to reflect the performance of their underlying components:

Price Weighting: In a price-weighted index, each stock's price per share determines its influence on the index's performance. The Dow Jones Industrial Average is a price-weighted index, where higher-priced stocks have a greater impact on the index's performance.

Market Capitalization Weighting: The most common method, market capitalization weighting, assigns weights to stocks based on their market value. This is calculated by multiplying the stock price by the number of outstanding shares. The S&P 500 uses market cap weighting, where larger companies have a larger impact on the index's performance.

Stock market indices are invaluable for various reasons

- **Benchmarking**: Investors use indices as benchmarks to compare the performance of their portfolios against the broader market or specific sectors. This helps gauge portfolio performance and identify areas of strength or weakness.
- **Diversification**: Investing in index funds or exchange-traded funds (ETFs) that track market indices allows investors to achieve broad diversification across a range of stocks or sectors without the need to individually select and manage each stock.
- **Market Analysis**: Analysts use index movements to assess market trends, economic conditions, and investor sentiment. Changes in index levels can signal shifts in market direction and provide insights into future market performance.
- **Investment Strategy**: Investors use indices to inform their investment decisions. For instance, an investor bullish on technology stocks may choose to allocate funds to an ETF tracking the NASDAQ Composite Index, which focuses on technology and growth stocks.

Stock market indices are foundational tools in finance, providing insights into market performance, benchmarks for investment portfolios, and guidance for investment strategies. Understanding the types of indices available, their calculation methods, and their applications in investment strategies allows investors to navigate the complexities of global financial markets effectively. By leveraging the information provided by indices, investors can make informed decisions to achieve their financial goals in a dynamic and ever-evolving economic landscape.

IPOs

An initial public offering (IPO) is a significant event for a company as it represents the first time the company's stock is publicly traded on a stock exchange. An IPO is a complex and highly regulated process, requiring significant planning and preparation from the company.

In this article, we will discuss the key steps involved in an IPO, the advantages and disadvantages of going public, and the factors that investors should consider when evaluating IPOs.

The IPO Process

The IPO process typically involves the following steps:

Step 1: Selecting an Underwriter

The first step in an IPO is to select an underwriter. An underwriter is an investment bank that assists the company in preparing the necessary documents, such as the prospectus, and helps the company to sell its shares to investors.

The underwriter typically charges a fee, which is a percentage of the total value of the shares sold. The underwriter may also purchase shares from the company and resell them to investors.

Step 2: Preparing the Prospectus

The prospectus is a document that provides investors with information about the company and its shares. The prospectus typically includes information about the company's history, operations, financial performance, and management team.

The prospectus is a critical document, and it must be reviewed and approved by the Securities and Exchange Commission (SEC) before the company can move forward with the IPO.

Step 3: Setting the Price

Before the IPO, the company and its underwriters must determine the price at which the shares will be sold to investors. This process typically involves a range of valuation techniques, such as discounted cash flow analysis and comparable company analysis.

The underwriter will then use this information to set the IPO price, which is the price at which the shares will be sold to investors. The IPO price is typically set based on a combination of the company's financial performance, industry trends, and the overall market conditions.

Step 4: Marketing the IPO

Once the IPO price has been set, the underwriter will market the IPO to potential investors. This typically involves a range of activities, such as roadshows, where the company's management team meets with investors to provide more information about the company.

The underwriter will also distribute the prospectus to potential investors and may use various marketing channels, such as social media, to generate interest in the IPO.

Step 5: Trading Begins

After the IPO price has been set and the shares have been sold to investors, trading of the company's shares will begin on the stock exchange. The price of the shares will be determined by the supply and demand for the shares on the open market.

Advantages and Disadvantages of Going Public

Going public through an IPO has several advantages and disadvantages that companies should consider before making a decision.

One of the most significant advantages of going public is the increased access to capital. By selling shares to the public, a company can raise a significant amount of capital that can be used to fund growth, expansion, or other strategic initiatives.

Going public can also enhance a company's credibility in the eyes of investors, customers, and suppliers. Being a public company requires a higher level of financial reporting and transparency, which can increase investor confidence in the company.

Going public also provides liquidity for shareholders. Once a company is publicly traded, its shares can be bought and sold on the open market, providing investors with an opportunity to cash out their investment.

Secondary Offerings

A secondary offering, in the context of the stock market, is when a company that is already publicly traded issues additional shares of its stock. The purpose of a secondary offering is typically to raise additional capital for the company, which can be used for various purposes such as funding growth initiatives, paying down debt, or making acquisitions.

When a company announces a secondary offering, it can have an impact on the stock's price and the broader stock market. If the market perceives the secondary offering as a positive development, such as a sign of the company's strong growth prospects, the stock price may rise. Conversely, if investors perceive the secondary offering as diluting the value of existing shares or a sign of financial weakness, the stock price may decline.

In general, secondary offerings are closely watched by investors and analysts because they can provide insights into the company's financial health and growth prospects. They can also indicate management's view of the company's future prospects and the level of investor interest in the company's stock.

Investors who own shares in a company that announces a secondary offering may have the opportunity to participate in the offering and purchase additional shares at a discounted price. However, this can also result in existing shares being diluted in value if the company issues a large number of new shares.

Secondary offerings can have a significant impact on a company's stock price and the broader stock market, and they are closely monitored by investors and analysts alike.

Stock Splits

A stock split is a corporate action that involves dividing existing shares of a company's stock into multiple shares. The purpose of a stock split is to increase the number of shares outstanding while decreasing the price per share, making the stock more affordable to a wider range of investors. This can also increase liquidity in the stock by making it easier to buy and sell shares.

In this article, we will discuss stock splits in more detail, including their history, the different types of stock splits, and the reasons why companies choose to split their stock. We will also examine the impact of stock splits on stock prices and the broader stock market.

History of Stock Splits

Stock splits have been a common corporate action for more than a century. In fact, the first stock split on record occurred in 1827, when the Bank of the United States split its stock 2-for-1. However, it wasn't until the early 20th century that stock splits became more common. The Standard Oil Company of New Jersey, for example, split its stock 4-for-1 in 1914, and the Ford Motor Company split its stock 3-for-1 in 1926.

Over the years, stock splits have become increasingly common as the stock market has grown and more companies have gone public. Today, stock splits are a routine corporate action for many publicly traded companies, especially those in the technology sector.

Types of Stock Splits

There are several types of stock splits that a company can choose to implement. The most common types include:

- ❖ 2-for-1 stock split: In a 2-for-1 stock split, each share of stock is split into two shares, effectively doubling the number of shares outstanding while halving the price per share.
- ❖ 3-for-1 stock split: In a 3-for-1 stock split, each share of stock is split into three shares, effectively tripling the number of shares outstanding while reducing the price per share to one-third of its previous level.
- ❖ 4-for-1 stock split: In a 4-for-1 stock split, each share of stock is split into four shares, effectively quadrupling the number of shares outstanding while reducing the price per share to one-fourth of its previous level.

Reverse stock split: In a reverse stock split, the number of outstanding shares is reduced, while the price per share is increased. For example, a company may implement a 1-for-2 reverse stock split, which would reduce the number of shares outstanding by half while doubling the price per share.

Reasons for Stock Splits

There are several reasons why a company may choose to implement a stock split. Some of the most common reasons include:

Making the stock more affordable: By reducing the price per share through a stock split, a company can make its stock more accessible to a wider range of investors. This can increase demand for the stock, which can drive up the price.

Increasing liquidity: A stock split can increase the number of shares outstanding, which can make it easier for investors to buy and sell shares. This can increase liquidity in the stock and make it more attractive to investors.

Attracting new investors: A stock split can also make a company's stock more attractive to new investors, who may be more willing to buy shares if they are more affordable.

Managing the price of the stock: Some companies may choose to implement a stock split in order to manage the price of the stock. For example, if a company's stock has risen to a very high price, it may implement a stock split to bring the price back down to a more manageable level.

Impact of Stock Splits on Stock Prices

Stock splits can have a significant impact on the price of a company's stock. While a stock split does not change the overall value of a company, it does change the number of outstanding shares and the price per share. This can affect the supply and demand of the stock, which can, in turn, impact the stock price.

In general, the announcement of a stock split is often seen as a positive development by investors, as it indicates that the company is growing and is confident in its future prospects. This can lead to an increase in demand for the stock, which can drive up the price in the short term.

However, the impact of a stock split on the stock price can vary depending on a number of factors, including the reason for the stock split, the overall market conditions, and investor sentiment towards the company.

If a company announces a stock split for a positive reason, such as to make the stock more affordable or to attract new investors, the stock price may rise in the short term. This is because the stock will become more accessible to a wider range of investors, which can increase demand for the stock and drive up the price.

However, if a company announces a stock split for a negative reason, such as to manage the price of the stock because it has become too high, the stock price may decline in the short term. This is because investors may view the stock split as a sign of weakness, which can lead to a decrease in demand for the stock and a decline in the price.

In addition, the impact of a stock split on the stock price can also depend on broader market conditions and investor sentiment towards the company. If the overall market is bullish and investors are optimistic about the company's future prospects, the stock price may rise more in response to a stock split. However, if the market is bearish or investors are cautious about the company's prospects, the impact of the stock split on the stock price may be more muted.

It is also worth noting that while a stock split can lead to an increase in demand for the stock in the short term, it does not necessarily indicate that the stock is a good long-term investment. Investors should always do their own research and analysis before investing in any stock, regardless of whether or not it has recently undergone a stock split.

Stock splits can have a significant impact on the price of a company's stock. While the announcement of a stock split is often seen as a positive development by investors, the impact on the stock price can vary depending on a number of factors, including the reason for the stock split, broader market conditions, and investor sentiment towards the company. Investors should always do their own research and analysis before investing in any stock, regardless of whether or not it has recently undergone a stock split.

In the world of corporate finance, a buyback, also known as a share repurchase, is a process by which a company buys back its own shares from the market. This is done by the company using its own funds to purchase the shares, which are then retired and no longer traded publicly. Buybacks have become increasingly popular in recent years, with many companies using them as a way to return excess cash to shareholders, boost earnings per share, and increase the value of their remaining shares.

How Buybacks Work

Share buybacks, a strategic financial maneuver employed by companies, involve repurchasing their own shares from the open market. This process typically begins with the company making a tender offer to its shareholders, offering to buy back shares at a premium to the current market price. By enticing shareholders to sell their shares back to the company, the goal is to reduce the number of outstanding shares in circulation.

Companies undertake share buybacks for several reasons. One primary motivation is to return excess cash to shareholders when the company has accumulated more funds than it needs for day-to-day operations or future growth initiatives. By repurchasing shares, the company effectively distributes cash back to shareholders, enhancing shareholder value and potentially boosting the price of the remaining shares by reducing their supply.

Another significant rationale for buybacks is to improve earnings per share (EPS). By reducing the number of shares outstanding, companies can increase EPS even if total earnings remain constant. This metric is critical for investors assessing a company's profitability and can make the stock more attractive in the market, potentially driving up its price.

Additionally, share buybacks can be used strategically to defend against hostile takeovers. By repurchasing a significant portion of its own shares, a company can make it more challenging for external parties to acquire a controlling stake, thereby safeguarding its independence and thwarting unwanted acquisition attempts.

However, the decision to engage in share buybacks is not without its criticisms and considerations. Critics argue that buybacks may represent a misallocation of capital, as funds used for repurchases could potentially be invested in research and development, employee wages, or other growth initiatives that could generate long-term value for the company.

Furthermore, some view buybacks as prioritizing short-term shareholder returns over long-term sustainability. By focusing on boosting EPS and share prices in the near term, companies may overlook investments in innovation or infrastructure that could drive future growth and competitive advantage.

Critics also raise concerns about buybacks artificially inflating stock prices, creating a perception of higher company value that may not be supported by underlying business fundamentals. This can lead to market distortions and overvaluation risks, potentially exposing investors to greater downside in market corrections.

Moreover, reducing cash reserves through buybacks can limit a company's financial flexibility. In times of economic uncertainty or market volatility, having ample cash on hand is crucial for navigating challenges, seizing growth opportunities, or funding unexpected needs.

While share buybacks can be an effective tool for enhancing shareholder value, boosting EPS, and defending against takeovers, they are subject to scrutiny and debate. Investors and stakeholders must carefully weigh the potential benefits and risks of buybacks, considering the company's long-term strategic objectives and its ability to balance shareholder returns with sustainable growth and financial resilience. Understanding the motivations, implications, and criticisms of share buybacks is essential for evaluating their impact on company performance and shareholder value over the long term.

CHAPTER 11

Bonds

Bonds are one of the most common types of investment vehicles available in financial markets today. A bond is a type of debt instrument that is issued by corporations, governments, and other entities to raise capital. When an investor purchases a bond, they are essentially lending money to the issuer, who promises to pay back the principal amount of the bond plus interest at a later date. Bonds are considered to be relatively low-risk investments, as the issuer is required to pay back the principal and interest to the investor.

Bonds can be a valuable addition to an investment portfolio, as they provide a source of income and can help to diversify a portfolio. Bonds can also be used to help manage risk, as they tend to have less volatility than stocks and can provide a steady source of income even during market downturns.

Types of Bonds

Bonds are financial instruments used by entities to raise capital. They are essentially a form of debt where the bond issuer promises to pay back the bondholder the principal amount, also known as face value, along with interest over a set period of time. Bonds are used by corporations, governments, and other entities as a way to finance their operations or special projects.

There are many different types of bonds available in the market, each with its own unique features and characteristics. Here are some of the most common types of bonds:

Treasury Bonds

Treasury bonds, also known as T-bonds, are issued by the US government to finance its operations. These bonds have a maturity period of 10 to 30 years and are considered to be the safest form of bond investment as they are backed by the full faith and credit of the US government.

Municipal Bonds

Municipal bonds are issued by state and local governments to finance projects such as schools, highways, and hospitals. These bonds are tax-exempt, which means that the interest income is not subject to federal income tax. They are typically issued with maturities of 20 to 30 years.

Corporate Bonds

Corporate bonds are issued by companies to finance their operations. They are riskier than government bonds as they are backed by the creditworthiness of the issuing company. Corporate bonds can be classified as investment-grade or high-yield, also known as junk bonds, depending on the credit rating of the issuing company.

International Bonds

International bonds, also known as global bonds, are issued by foreign governments and corporations. These bonds are typically denominated in a major currency such as US dollars or euro and are subject to the credit risk of the issuing entity as well as currency risk.

Zero-Coupon Bonds

Zero-coupon bonds are bonds that do not pay periodic interest. Instead, they are issued at a discount to their face value and pay out the full face value at maturity. Because they do not pay interest, they are often sold at a deep discount to their face value and can be purchased at a significant discount to their maturity value.

Floating Rate Bonds

Floating rate bonds are bonds that have a variable interest rate. The interest rate is typically tied to a benchmark rate such as LIBOR or the prime rate and changes periodically based on the movement of the benchmark rate. These bonds are often used by investors who want to protect themselves against rising interest rates.

Inflation-Linked Bonds

Inflation-linked bonds, also known as inflation-indexed bonds, are bonds where the principal and interest payments are adjusted for inflation. These bonds are often issued by governments to help protect against inflation and provide a hedge against rising prices.

Convertible Bonds

Convertible bonds are bonds that can be converted into a specified number of shares of the issuing company's common stock. These bonds are often issued by companies with high growth potential and offer investors the opportunity to participate in the upside potential of the company's stock while still providing a fixed income stream.

Callable Bonds

Callable bonds are bonds that can be called, or redeemed, by the issuing company before the maturity date. These bonds typically have higher yields than non-callable bonds, as the issuer has the right to redeem the bond if interest rates decline, which can leave investors with lower returns.

Junk Bonds

Junk bonds are high-yield bonds that are issued by companies with a lower credit rating. These bonds are considered to be riskier than investment-grade bonds and offer higher yields to compensate for the increased risk. Junk bonds are often issued by companies with a high level of debt or by companies in distressed industries.

When discussing the types of bonds and their characteristics, some concepts can be technically complex and might benefit from visualization for clearer understanding. Here's how you can represent this information in a table format to make it easier to grasp, especially focusing on aspects like interest payments and risk levels which are fundamental but can be challenging to understand:

Bond Type	Interest Mechanism	Risk Level	Typical Investors
Treasury Bonds	Fixed interest over 10-30 years	Very Low	Risk-averse investors looking for safety
Municipal Bonds	Often tax-exempt fixed interest	Low to Moderate	Tax-conscious investors, risk-averse individuals
Corporate Bonds	Fixed or variable interest	Varies (Low to High)	Diverse, from conservative to risk-tolerant investors
International Bonds	Currency-based interest rates	Moderate to High	Investors seeking diversity and higher risk/reward
Zero-Coupon Bonds	No periodic interest; lump-sum at maturity	Moderate to High	Investors seeking long-term growth without immediate returns
Floating Rate Bonds	Variable rates tied to benchmarks like LIBOR	Moderate	Investors looking to hedge against interest rate fluctuations
Inflation-Linked Bonds	Interest adjusts with inflation rates	Low to Moderate	Investors looking for protection against inflation
Convertible Bonds	Fixed interest, convertible to stock	Moderate to High	Investors interested in both bonds and potential stock gains
Callable Bonds	Fixed interest, but can be redeemed early by issuer	Moderate to High	Investors willing to accept higher risk for potentially higher yields
Junk Bonds	High interest to compensate for higher risk	High	Investors seeking high returns at higher risk levels

This table simplifies complex bond features into key attributes like the type of interest mechanism and risk level, along with typical investor profiles. Understanding these can help investors match their risk tolerance and investment goals with the right type of bond:

Interest Mechanism: This column explains how interest is paid on each bond type, highlighting differences between fixed, variable, and non-periodic payments.

Risk Level: Indicates the general risk associated with each type of bond, helping investors understand potential downsides.

Typical Investors: Describes the types of investors who typically invest in these bonds, providing insight into who might prefer certain types of bonds based on their investment strategy and risk tolerance.

Bond Pricing

Bond pricing is a critical financial process used to determine the current market value of a bond. This market value is derived from the bond's anticipated future cash flows, including both the principal repayment at maturity and the interest payments made throughout the bond's life. To calculate this value, these future cash flows are discounted back to their present value using a discount rate that reflects both the time value of money and the specific risk characteristics of the bond.

The basic formula to calculate the price of a bond is as follows:

$$\text{Bond Price} = \left(\frac{\text{Coupon Payment}}{\text{Discount Rate}} \right) \times \left[1 - \frac{1}{(1+\text{Discount Rate})^n} \right] + \frac{\text{Face Value}}{(1+\text{Discount Rate})^n}$$

- **Coupon Payment**: This is the periodic interest payment the bond issuer makes to the bondholder. For instance, a bond with a $1,000 face value and a 5% coupon rate will pay $50 annually in interest. This payment is integral in calculating the present value of expected interest payments from the bond.
- **Discount Rate**: Also known as the required rate of return, this rate is what investors demand as a return on their investment in the bond. It reflects the perceived risk level of the bond and the broader market conditions. A lower perceived risk leads to a lower discount rate and thus a higher bond price, while a higher perceived risk leads to a higher discount rate and a lower bond price.
- **n**: This represents the number of periods until the bond matures. The further away the maturity, the more the future cash flows must be discounted back to their present value.
- **Face Value**: This is the amount promised by the issuer to pay the bondholder at the bond's maturity. It is also known as the principal amount of the bond.

89

The interplay between these factors—how much and how often interest is paid (coupon payment), the maturity length (n), and the required return (discount rate)—directly influences a bond's price. For instance, if market interest rates rise, the discount rates will increase, leading to a decrease in bond prices, and vice versa.

Understanding bond pricing is crucial for investors aiming to optimize their portfolios for both risk and return, ensuring alignment with their broader financial strategies and market outlook. This pricing mechanism provides a clear, quantifiable measure of a bond's worth at any given time based on its expected future cash flows discounted back to their current value.

Number of Periods

The number of periods remaining until the bond matures is also a key component of bond pricing. This is because the present value of future cash flows decreases as the time horizon lengthens. Therefore, bonds with longer maturities will have a lower present value than bonds with shorter maturities.

Face Value The face value, also known as the par value, is the amount that the bond issuer promises to pay back at maturity. The face value is used to calculate the present value of the bond's principal repayment.

Once these components are determined, the bond price can be calculated using the above formula. It's important to note that bond prices are also influenced by other factors such as prevailing interest rates, inflation expectations, credit ratings, and market demand. As a result, bond prices are subject to change over time.

Yield

Yield is a measure of the income that an investor can expect to receive from an investment, expressed as a percentage of the investment's cost or current market value. Yield is a crucial metric for investors in fixed income securities such as bonds, and it can also be used to evaluate the income potential of dividend-paying stocks, real estate investment trusts (REITs), and other income-generating investments.

There are several types of yield, including current yield, yield to maturity, yield to call, and yield to worst. Each of these measures provides a different perspective on the income potential of a particular investment.

Current Yield Current yield is the simplest measure of yield and is calculated by dividing the annual interest or dividend payment by the current market price of the investment. For example, if a bond pays a coupon of $50 per year and is currently trading at $1,000, the current yield would be 5%. Current yield is often used as a quick and easy way to compare the income potential of different fixed income securities.

90

Yield to Maturity Yield to maturity (YTM) is the total return that an investor can expect to receive if the bond is held until maturity. YTM takes into account the present value of all future cash flows, including interest payments and the return of principal at maturity. YTM is calculated using a complex formula that incorporates the bond's coupon rate, time to maturity, and current market price. In general, the YTM of a bond will be higher than its current yield if the bond is trading at a discount to its face value and lower than its current yield if the bond is trading at a premium.

Yield to Call Yield to call (YTC) is similar to yield to maturity, but it takes into account the possibility that the bond may be called or redeemed by the issuer before its maturity date. YTC is the total return that an investor can expect if the bond is called at the earliest possible call date. YTC is generally calculated in the same way as YTM, but it also takes into account the call price, call date, and call premium, if any.

Yield to Worst Yield to worst (YTW) is the lowest yield that an investor can expect to receive if certain adverse events occur, such as the bond being called or the issuer defaulting. YTW is calculated by assuming that the bond will be called or defaulted on at the earliest possible date, which results in the lowest possible yield. YTW is often used as a measure of the downside risk of a bond investment.

Yield can also be affected by a variety of factors such as interest rates, credit risk, inflation, and market conditions. For example, if interest rates rise, the yield on existing bonds will become less attractive, causing their market value to decline. Similarly, if the creditworthiness of the issuer deteriorates, the yield on its bonds will increase to compensate investors for the increased risk.

CHAPTER 12

ETFs

Exchange-traded funds (ETFs) are investment funds that are traded on stock exchanges, much like individual stocks. ETFs are designed to track the performance of a particular index, such as the S&P 500, or to represent a particular sector or asset class, such as technology stocks or gold. ETFs have become increasingly popular among investors due to their low fees, tax efficiency, and ease of trading.

History of ETFs The first ETF, the SPDR S&P 500 ETF, was launched in 1993 by State Street Global Advisors. Since then, the ETF market has grown rapidly, and there are now thousands of ETFs available to investors, covering a wide range of asset classes and investment strategies. In addition to traditional index-tracking ETFs, there are also actively managed ETFs that use a variety of investment strategies to outperform the market.

How ETFs Work ETFs are similar to mutual funds in that they are pooled investment vehicles that provide investors with exposure to a diversified portfolio of assets. However, there are several key differences between ETFs and mutual funds. One of the main differences is that ETFs are traded on stock exchanges, which means that investors can buy and sell them throughout the trading day, just like individual stocks. Mutual funds, on the other hand, can only be bought or sold at the end of the trading day, after the net asset value (NAV) of the fund has been calculated.

Another key difference between ETFs and mutual funds is that ETFs are typically passively managed, which means that they seek to track the performance of a particular index or benchmark. This is in contrast to actively managed mutual funds, which have a portfolio manager who actively selects and manages the fund's holdings in an attempt to outperform the market.

Benefits of ETFs ETFs have become increasingly popular among investors due to their many benefits. Some of the key benefits of ETFs include:

- **Low fees:** ETFs typically have lower fees than mutual funds, making them an attractive option for cost-conscious investors.
- **Tax efficiency:** ETFs are generally more tax efficient than mutual funds, because they are structured as pass-through entities and do not have to sell securities to meet redemptions, which can trigger capital gains taxes.
- **Diversification:** ETFs provide investors with exposure to a diversified portfolio of assets, which can help to reduce portfolio risk.
- **Transparency:** ETFs are highly transparent, because they disclose their holdings on a daily basis. This allows investors to know exactly what they are investing in.
- **Flexibility:** ETFs can be bought and sold throughout the trading day, which provides investors with greater flexibility than mutual funds.

Types of ETFs

Exchange-traded funds (ETFs) are investment funds that trade on stock exchanges and are designed to track the performance of a particular index, sector, or asset class. There are many different types of ETFs available to investors, each with its own investment objective and strategy. Some of the most common types of ETFs are:

Equity ETFs: Equity ETFs invest in stocks and are designed to track the performance of a particular stock index, such as the S&P 500. Equity ETFs are the most popular type of ETF and account for the majority of ETF assets.

Fixed income ETFs: Fixed income ETFs invest in bonds and other fixed-income securities, such as treasury bonds, corporate bonds, and municipal bonds. These ETFs are designed to provide investors with income and capital preservation.

Commodity ETFs: Commodity ETFs invest in commodities such as gold, oil, and agricultural products. These ETFs are designed to provide investors with exposure to commodity prices.

Currency ETFs: Currency ETFs invest in currencies, such as the US dollar, euro, or Japanese yen, and are designed to provide investors with exposure to foreign exchange rates.

Real estate ETFs: Real estate ETFs invest in real estate investment trusts (REITs), which are companies that own and manage income-producing real estate properties. These ETFs are designed to provide investors with exposure to the real estate market.

Sector ETFs: Sector ETFs invest in a particular sector of the economy, such as technology, healthcare, or energy. These ETFs are designed to provide investors with exposure to specific industries or sectors.

International ETFs: International ETFs invest in stocks and bonds from foreign countries, and are designed to provide investors with exposure to international markets. These ETFs can be broad-based, such as an ETF that invests in all stocks listed on a particular foreign exchange, or they can be country-specific, such as an ETF that invests only in stocks listed on the Japanese stock exchange.

Smart beta ETFs: Smart beta ETFs are a type of ETF that seeks to outperform the market by using a rules-based approach to selecting and weighting stocks. Smart beta ETFs can be designed to outperform the market by selecting stocks based on factors such as value, momentum, or quality.

Thematic ETFs: Thematic ETFs invest in companies that are focused on a particular theme or trend, such as renewable energy, blockchain technology, or artificial intelligence. Thematic ETFs are designed to provide investors with exposure to companies that are positioned to benefit from a particular trend or theme.

Active ETFs: Active ETFs are a type of ETF that are actively managed by a portfolio manager who selects and manages the fund's holdings in an attempt to outperform the market. Active ETFs are a relatively new type of ETF, and they have gained popularity in recent years as investors have sought out low-cost alternatives to traditional actively managed mutual funds.

Inverse ETFs: Inverse ETFs are a type of ETF that are designed to profit from a decline in the value of the underlying index or asset class. Inverse ETFs use various derivatives to achieve their inverse exposure, and they are generally used by investors as a way to hedge against market declines.

Leveraged ETFs: Leveraged ETFs are a type of ETF that use derivatives to provide leveraged exposure to the underlying index or asset class. Leveraged ETFs are designed to provide investors with enhanced returns in a rising market, but they can also amplify losses in a declining market.

ESG ETFs: ESG (environmental, social, and governance) ETFs invest in companies that meet certain environmental, social, and governance criteria.

Understanding ETFs with a Table

ETF Type	Objective	Common Investments
Equity ETFs	Track stock indices	Stocks in various indices
Fixed Income ETFs	Generate income	Bonds, treasuries, municipal bonds
Commodity ETFs	Hedge or gain from commodity prices	Physical commodities like gold or oil

ETF Type	Objective	Common Investments
Currency ETFs	Exposure to forex movements	Various global currencies
Real Estate ETFs	Invest in real estate	REITs owning real property
Sector ETFs	Invest in specific economic sectors	Stocks in selected sectors
International ETFs	Diversify internationally	Stocks and bonds from non-domestic markets
Smart Beta ETFs	Outperform market indices	Stocks chosen based on factors like volatility, dividends
Thematic ETFs	Capitalize on trends	Companies driving or benefiting from trends
Active ETFs	Outperform benchmarks	Actively managed portfolio selections
Inverse ETFs	Profit from declines in indices	Derivatives for short positions
Leveraged ETFs	Amplify returns	Derivatives to increase exposure to an index
ESG ETFs	Invest in ethically responsible companies	Companies meeting specific ESG criteria

ETFs vs. Mutual Funds

Exchange-traded funds (ETFs) and mutual funds are both investment vehicles that provide investors with exposure to a diversified portfolio of stocks, bonds, or other assets. However, there are some key differences between ETFs and mutual funds that make them more or less suitable for different types of investors. Here are some of the key differences between ETFs and mutual funds:

ETFs vs. Mutual Funds

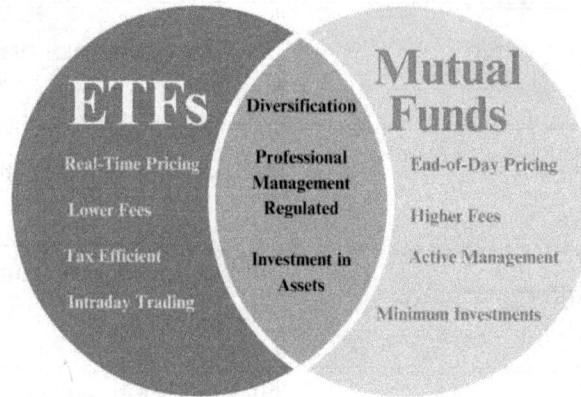

ETFs
- Real-Time Pricing
- Lower Fees
- Tax Efficient
- Intraday Trading

(overlap) Diversification, Professional Management, Regulated, Investment in Assets

Mutual Funds
- End-of-Day Pricing
- Higher Fees
- Active Management
- Minimum Investments

Trading

ETFs are traded on stock exchanges, just like individual stocks, and their prices fluctuate throughout the day based on market demand. Mutual funds, on the other hand, are priced only once per day, after the market has closed. This means that ETFs offer more flexibility in terms of trading, allowing investors to buy and sell them throughout the trading day.

Costs

ETFs tend to have lower expense ratios than mutual funds, which can make them a more cost-effective investment option. This is because ETFs are generally passively managed, meaning they track a specific index, and have lower operating costs than actively managed mutual funds. Additionally, ETFs can be bought and sold like stocks, so there are no sales charges or redemption fees.

Minimum investment

Many mutual funds require a minimum investment to get started, which can be a barrier for smaller investors. ETFs, on the other hand, can be purchased for the price of a single share, making them more accessible to a wider range of investors.

Tax efficiency

ETFs tend to be more tax efficient than mutual funds, because they are structured in a way that allows investors to minimize their tax liabilities. ETFs are able to avoid capital gains taxes by using an in-kind redemption process, which allows investors to exchange shares of the ETF for a basket of securities that closely match the ETF's holdings.

Diversification

Both ETFs and mutual funds provide investors with a diversified portfolio of stocks, bonds, or other assets, which can help reduce risk. However, ETFs may offer greater diversification because they can track a wider range of indexes or asset classes.

Transparency

ETFs are generally more transparent than mutual funds, because they are required to disclose their holdings on a daily basis. This can be helpful for investors who want to know exactly what they are investing in.

Active vs. passive management

While both ETFs and mutual funds can be actively managed or passively managed, the majority of ETFs are passively managed. This means that they track a specific index and do not rely on the expertise of a portfolio manager to select individual securities. Mutual funds, on the other hand, can be actively managed or passively managed, depending on the investment strategy of the fund.

CHAPTER 13

Index Funds

An index fund is a type of mutual fund or exchange-traded fund (ETF) that seeks to replicate the performance of a particular stock market index, such as the S&P 500 or the Dow Jones Industrial Average. Index funds are designed to provide investors with low-cost, diversified exposure to a broad range of stocks, with the aim of achieving returns that match or closely approximate the overall performance of the index.

Index funds were first introduced in the 1970s by John Bogle, the founder of the Vanguard Group, who recognized that many actively managed mutual funds were not able to consistently outperform the market. Bogle believed that the key to long-term investment success was to keep costs low and focus on the long-term trends of the overall market, rather than trying to beat it by picking individual stocks.

Index funds have become increasingly popular over the past few decades, as investors have come to recognize the benefits of low-cost, passive investing.

How Index Funds Work

Index funds work by attempting to replicate the performance of a particular stock market index, such as the S&P 500 or the Dow Jones Industrial Average. The index fund invests in a portfolio of stocks that mirrors the composition of the underlying index, with the goal of achieving returns that match or closely approximate the overall performance of the index.

The portfolio of stocks held by an index fund is typically determined by the weighting of the individual stocks in the underlying index. For example, if a particular stock accounts for 3% of the total market capitalization of the S&P 500, then the index fund will hold a 3% allocation of that stock in its portfolio.

Because index funds are designed to provide broad market exposure, they are often diversified across a wide range of sectors and companies, which can help to reduce risk by spreading investments across multiple stocks.

Index funds can be either mutual funds or exchange-traded funds (ETFs). Mutual funds are pooled investment vehicles that allow investors to purchase shares of the fund, with the fund manager using the pooled funds to buy a portfolio of stocks. ETFs are traded on an exchange like individual stocks, and investors can buy or sell shares of the ETF throughout the day, rather than just at the end of the trading day like with mutual funds.

One of the key advantages of index funds is their low cost. Because index funds are designed to track the performance of an underlying index, they typically require less management and analysis than actively managed funds, which can result in lower fees for investors.

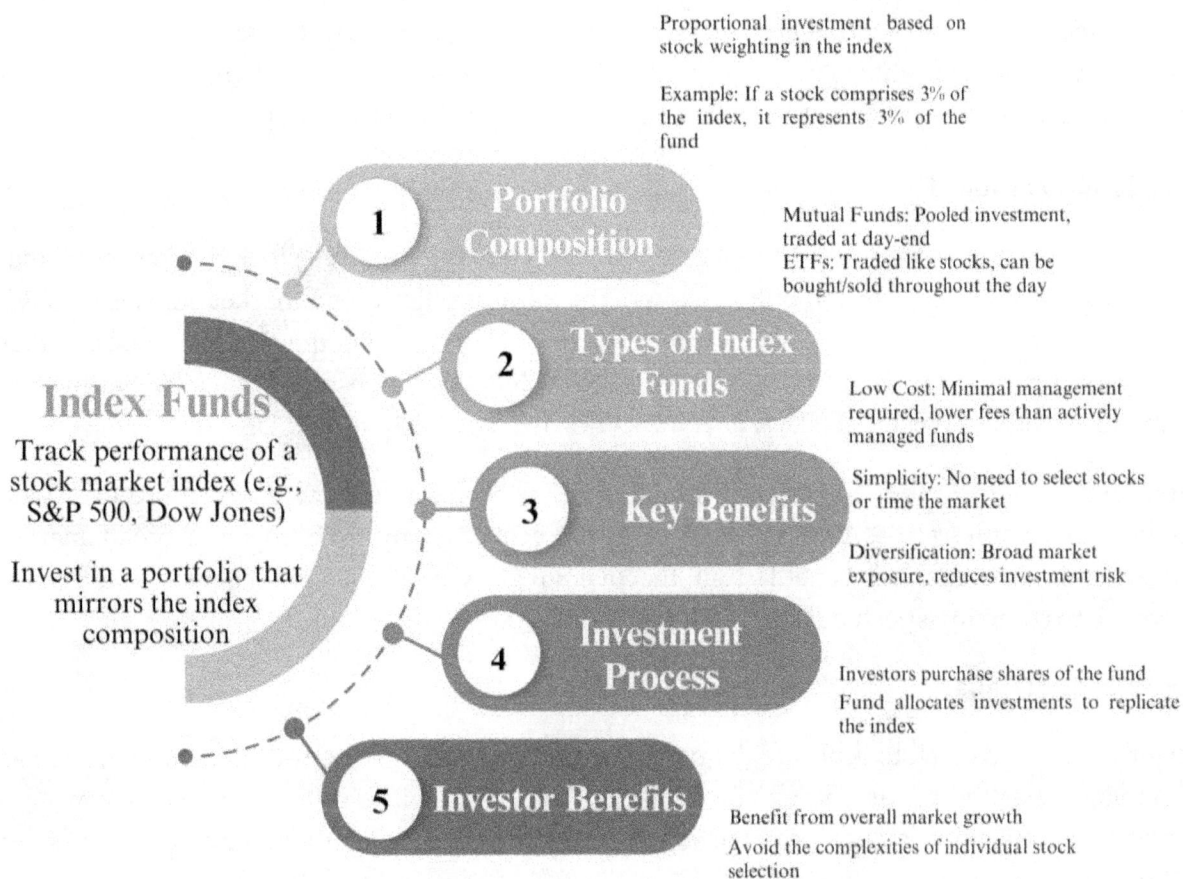

Proportional investment based on stock weighting in the index

Example: If a stock comprises 3% of the index, it represents 3% of the fund

1 Portfolio Composition

Mutual Funds: Pooled investment, traded at day-end
ETFs: Traded like stocks, can be bought/sold throughout the day

Index Funds

Track performance of a stock market index (e.g., S&P 500, Dow Jones)

Invest in a portfolio that mirrors the index composition

2 Types of Index Funds

Low Cost: Minimal management required, lower fees than actively managed funds

Simplicity: No need to select stocks or time the market

3 Key Benefits

Diversification: Broad market exposure, reduces investment risk

4 Investment Process

Investors purchase shares of the fund
Fund allocates investments to replicate the index

5 Investor Benefits

Benefit from overall market growth
Avoid the complexities of individual stock selection

Another advantage of index funds is their simplicity. Because index funds seek to track a particular index, investors do not need to worry about selecting individual stocks or timing the market. Instead, they can simply invest in an index fund and benefit from the overall growth of the market over time.

To illustrate how an index fund works, consider an investor who wants to invest in the S&P 500 index. The investor could purchase shares in an S&P 500 index fund, which would hold a portfolio of stocks that mirrors the composition of the S&P 500 index. The investor would benefit from the overall growth of the market, without having to worry about the performance of individual stocks.

Index funds work by attempting to replicate the performance of a particular stock market index, providing investors with low-cost, diversified exposure to a broad range of stocks. By investing in an index fund, investors can benefit from the overall growth of the market, without having to worry about selecting individual stocks or timing the market.

Types of Index Funds

Index funds are a type of passive investment that aims to replicate the performance of a specific stock market index. As such, there are many different types of index funds that investors can choose from, each of which provides exposure to a different segment of the market. In this article, we'll take a closer look at the different types of index funds available to investors.

Broad Market Index Funds

Broad market index funds seek to replicate the performance of a large stock market index that represents a broad cross-section of the market. The most popular broad market index is the S&P 500, which tracks the 500 largest publicly traded companies in the United States. Other examples of broad market indexes include the Russell 3000, which tracks the 3,000 largest US companies, and the Wilshire 5000, which tracks nearly all publicly traded US stocks.

Broad market index funds are an attractive option for investors who want exposure to a wide range of companies across different sectors of the economy. By investing in a broad market index fund, investors can benefit from the overall growth of the market and reduce their exposure to company-specific risks.

Sector Index Funds

Sector index funds seek to replicate the performance of a specific sector of the economy, such as technology, healthcare, or energy. By investing in a sector index fund, investors can gain exposure to the performance of a particular industry or sector without having to invest in individual companies.

Sector index funds can be useful for investors who want to invest in a particular industry or who believe that a certain sector will outperform the broader market. However, it's worth noting that investing in a sector index fund is riskier than investing in a broad market index fund, as the performance of the sector may be more volatile.

International Index Funds

International index funds seek to replicate the performance of a stock market index in a foreign country or region. Examples of international indexes include the MSCI EAFE (Europe, Australasia, Far East), which tracks stocks in developed countries outside of North America, and the MSCI Emerging Markets, which tracks stocks in emerging market economies.

International index funds can provide investors with exposure to companies and economies outside of their home country, which can help to diversify their portfolio and reduce their exposure to currency risk. However, it's worth noting that investing in international index funds carries additional risks, including political instability, currency fluctuations, and regulatory differences.

Bond Index Funds

Bond index funds seek to replicate the performance of a fixed-income index, such as the Bloomberg Barclays Aggregate Bond Index. Bond index funds invest in a portfolio of bonds that mirrors the composition of the underlying index, with the goal of achieving returns that match or closely approximate the overall performance of the index.

Bond index funds can be an attractive option for investors who want exposure to the fixed-income market without having to select individual bonds. Bond index funds can also help to diversify a portfolio and provide a source of steady income.

Commodity Index Funds

Commodity index funds seek to replicate the performance of a commodity index, such as the S&P GSCI Commodity Index. These funds invest in a portfolio of commodities, such as oil, gold, or agricultural products, with the goal of achieving returns that match or closely approximate the overall performance of the index.

Commodity index funds can be an attractive option for investors who want exposure to the commodity market without having to purchase physical commodities. However, it's worth noting that investing in commodity index funds can be more volatile than investing in other types of index funds, as the prices of commodities can be highly sensitive to supply and demand factors.

Style Index Funds

Style index funds seek to replicate the performance of a particular investment style, such as value or growth. Value stocks are those that are considered undervalued by the market.

Type of Index Fund	Overview	Key Considerations
Broad Market Index Funds	Track a large stock market index, such as the S&P 500, Russell 3000, or Wilshire 5000, representing a broad cross-section of companies.	Offers diversified exposure, reduces company-specific risk, and reflects overall market growth. Suitable for long-term investors.
Sector Index Funds	Focus on a specific industry or sector, such as technology, healthcare, or energy.	Provides targeted exposure but carries higher risk due to sector volatility. Best for investors with strong conviction in a particular sector.
International Index Funds	Track stock market indexes from foreign countries or regions, such as MSCI EAFE or MSCI Emerging Markets.	Offers global diversification but carries additional risks like currency fluctuations, political instability, and regulatory differences.
Bond Index Funds	Replicate the performance of fixed-income indexes, such as the Bloomberg Barclays Aggregate Bond Index, by investing in a mix of bonds.	Provides income and portfolio stability. Less volatile than stock funds but sensitive to interest rate changes.
Commodity Index Funds	Invest in a basket of commodities like oil, gold, or agricultural products, tracking indexes like the S&P GSCI Commodity Index.	Offers exposure to commodity markets, useful for inflation hedging but subject to high price volatility.
Style Index Funds	Focus on specific investment styles such as value stocks (undervalued companies) or growth stocks (high-potential companies).	Helps investors align with their preferred investing strategy. Can be cyclical, performing well in certain market conditions.

Index funds have become increasingly popular with investors in recent years, as they offer a low-cost, passive approach to investing that can provide exposure to a wide range of securities. However, like any investment product, there are pros and cons to investing in index funds. In this article, we'll take a closer look at the advantages and disadvantages of index funds.

Pros of Index Funds

Low Fees

One of the primary advantages of index funds is their low fees. Because they are passively managed, index funds don't require the same level of research and analysis as actively managed funds, which can lead to lower costs for investors. In addition, because index funds are designed to replicate the performance of a specific index, there is no need for frequent buying and selling of securities, which can also help to keep costs low.

Diversification

Another advantage of index funds is that they offer diversification across a broad range of securities. For example, a broad market index fund like the S&P 500 can provide exposure to hundreds of different companies across different sectors of the economy. This diversification can help to reduce the risk of investing in any single security and can help to improve overall portfolio performance.

Simplicity

Index funds are also relatively simple to understand and invest in. Because they are designed to replicate the performance of a specific index, there is no need to spend time researching individual securities or trying to time the market. This simplicity can be especially attractive to investors who are new to investing or who don't have the time or expertise to manage their investments actively.

Tax Efficiency

Index funds can be more tax-efficient than actively managed funds because they typically have lower turnover. This means that there are fewer taxable events, such as capital gains, that can trigger taxes for investors. In addition, because index funds are designed to replicate the performance of a specific index, there is less need for buying and selling of securities, which can also help to reduce the tax impact on investors.

Cons of Index Funds

Limited Upside Potential

One of the primary disadvantages of index funds is that they are designed to replicate the performance of a specific index, which means that they are unlikely to outperform the market. While this can be an advantage in terms of reducing risk, it also means that investors are unlikely to see significant upside potential beyond the performance of the index.

Lack of Control

Another disadvantage of index funds is that investors have little control over the securities that are included in the fund. Because index funds are designed to replicate the performance of a specific index, there is no opportunity to pick and choose individual securities or to adjust the allocation of the portfolio. This lack of control can be a disadvantage for investors who want to customize their portfolio to meet their specific investment goals.

Exposure to Underperforming Securities

Index funds are designed to replicate the performance of a specific index, which means that they may include securities that are underperforming or experiencing financial difficulties. While this exposure can help to reduce risk through diversification, it can also mean that investors are exposed to the underperformance of individual securities or sectors.

Vulnerability to Market Changes

Index funds are also vulnerable to changes in the market, as they are designed to replicate the performance of a specific index. If the underlying index experiences a significant downturn, so too will the index fund. While diversification can help to reduce risk, it cannot eliminate the risk of market volatility.

CHAPTER 14

Dividends

Dividends are a form of payment that companies make to their shareholders as a way to share profits. They are one of the most common ways for investors to receive returns on their investment, and many investors consider them to be an important part of their investment strategy. In this article, we'll take a closer look at dividends, including what they are, how they work, and why companies pay them.

What Are Dividends?

Dividends are payments that companies make to their shareholders as a way to share their profits. They are typically paid in cash, although some companies may choose to pay dividends in the form of additional shares of stock. Dividends are usually paid out on a regular basis, such as quarterly or annually, although the exact frequency of dividend payments can vary from company to company.

How Do Dividends Work?

When a company earns a profit, it can choose to use that money in a number of ways. It can reinvest the profits back into the company in order to fuel growth, it can pay down debt, or it can choose to pay out a portion of the profits to its shareholders in the form of dividends. The decision to pay dividends is typically made by the company's board of directors, and the amount of the dividend payment is usually determined by the company's earnings and financial position.

Dividend payments are typically expressed as a dividend yield, which is the annual dividend payment as a percentage of the stock price. For example, if a company pays a $2 dividend on a stock that is trading at $50 per share, the dividend yield would be 4%. The dividend yield can be a useful metric for investors who are comparing different stocks and trying to determine which ones offer the best potential return on their investment.

Why Do Companies Pay Dividends?

There are several reasons why companies might choose to pay dividends to their shareholders. One of the most common reasons is to reward shareholders for their investment in the company. By paying dividends, companies can encourage investors to hold onto their shares and to continue to invest in the company over the long term.

Another reason why companies might pay dividends is to signal to the market that the company is financially stable and has strong earnings potential. Companies that pay dividends on a regular basis are often viewed as being financially healthy and well-managed, which can help to attract new investors and support the company's stock price.

Finally, some companies may choose to pay dividends as a way to reduce their tax burden. In some cases, companies can receive a tax deduction for the amount of dividends that they pay to their shareholders. This can help to lower the company's tax bill and provide additional financial benefits to both the company and its shareholders.

Types of Dividends

Dividends are a way for companies to share profits with their shareholders, and they come in several different forms. In this article, we'll take a closer look at the different types of dividends that companies may offer, including cash dividends, stock dividends, property dividends, and special dividends.

Cash Dividends

Cash dividends are the most common type of dividend, and they are what most people think of when they hear the term "dividend." A cash dividend is a payment that a company makes to its shareholders in the form of cash. The amount of the cash dividend is typically expressed as a dollar amount per share, such as $0.50 per share. The company will determine the amount of the cash dividend based on its earnings and financial position.

Cash dividends are typically paid out on a regular basis, such as quarterly or annually, although the exact frequency of dividend payments can vary from company to company. Companies that pay cash dividends on a regular basis are often viewed as being financially healthy and well-managed, which can help to attract new investors and support the company's stock price.

Stock Dividends

A stock dividend is a dividend that is paid out in the form of additional shares of stock, rather than in cash. When a company issues a stock dividend, it will typically distribute a certain number of additional shares to its shareholders based on the number of shares that they already own. For example, if a company issues a 10% stock dividend and a shareholder owns 100 shares of the company's stock, they will receive an additional 10 shares.

Stock dividends can be a way for companies to reward their shareholders without using cash, which can be particularly useful for companies that may be facing cash flow issues or that want to conserve their cash for other purposes. Stock dividends can also be a way for companies to signal to the market that they believe their stock is undervalued, since the additional shares can increase the liquidity and trading volume of the stock.

Property Dividends

A property dividend is a dividend that is paid out in the form of property, rather than in cash or stock. Property dividends can take many forms, including physical assets such as real estate or equipment, or intangible assets such as patents or copyrights.

Property dividends are relatively rare, since they can be difficult to value and distribute to shareholders. They are most commonly used by companies that have significant assets that are not being fully utilized or that are difficult to sell, such as real estate or intellectual property.

Special Dividends

A special dividend is a one-time dividend payment that a company makes to its shareholders, in addition to any regular dividends that it may pay. Special dividends are typically paid out when a company has a large amount of excess cash on hand, or when it has sold off a major asset or received a windfall of cash from another source.

Special dividends can be a way for companies to reward their shareholders for their investment in the company, and they can also be a way to signal to the market that the company is financially strong and well-managed. Special dividends can also be a way to avoid the negative consequences of hoarding excess cash, such as lower stock prices or increased pressure from investors to deploy the cash in other ways.

How Dividends are paid

Dividends are a way for companies to share profits with their shareholders, and they can be paid out in a variety of ways in this section we'll take a closer look at the different methods that companies may use to pay dividends, including cash dividends, stock dividends, and dividend reinvestment plans.

How Dividends are paid

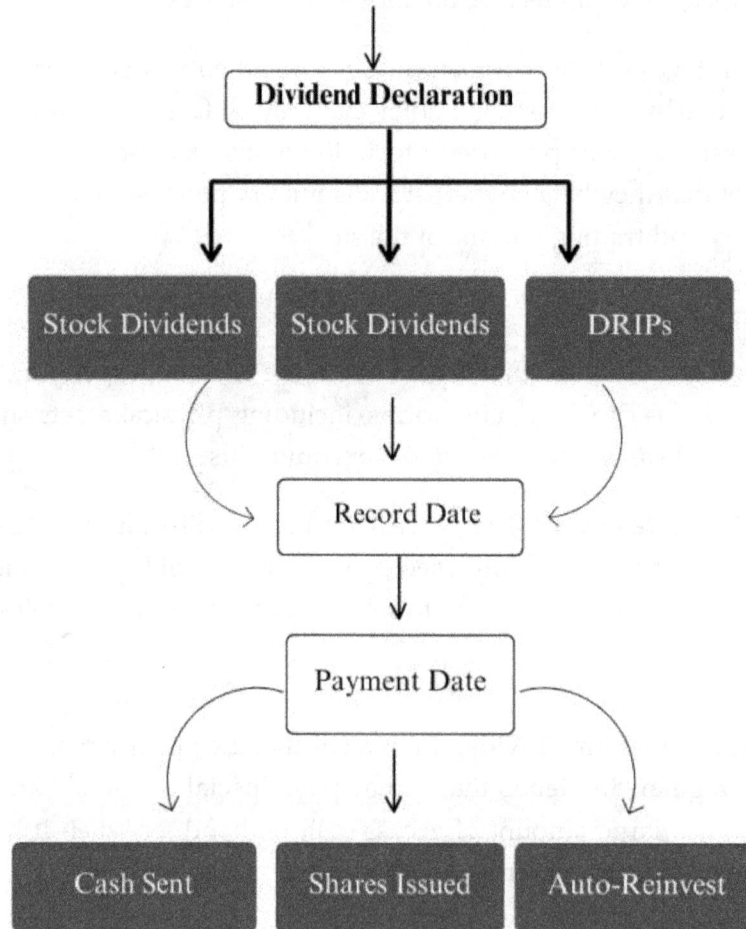

```
                    Dividend Declaration
         ┌───────────────┬───────────────┐
         ▼               ▼               ▼
  ┌──────────────┐ ┌──────────────┐ ┌──────────┐
  │Stock Dividends│ │Stock Dividends│ │  DRIPs   │
  └──────────────┘ └──────────────┘ └──────────┘
         │               │               │
         └──────────┐    ▼    ┌──────────┘
                ┌─────────────┐
                │ Record Date │
                └─────────────┘
                       │
                       ▼
                ┌─────────────┐
                │Payment Date │
                └─────────────┘
         ┌──────────┼──────────┐
         ▼          ▼          ▼
  ┌──────────┐┌──────────┐┌──────────────┐
  │Cash Sent ││Shares    ││Auto-Reinvest │
  │          ││Issued    ││              │
  └──────────┘└──────────┘└──────────────┘
```

Cash Dividends

Cash dividends are the most common type of dividend, distributed as cash payments to shareholders. The amount is typically expressed as a dollar value per share (e.g., $0.50 per share), determined by the company's earnings and financial health. Below is a structured breakdown of key aspects:

No.	Aspect	Details
1	Type	Cash payments to shareholders.
2	Expression	Dollar amount per share (e.g., $0.50).
3	Determination	Based on company earnings and financial position.
4	Frequency	Typically quarterly or annually; varies by company.

No.	Aspect	Details
5	**Benefits**	Signals financial stability, attracts investors, and supports stock price.
6	**Eligibility Requirement**	Shareholders must own the stock on the **record date** (cut-off date for eligibility).
7	**Payment Date**	Date when cash is disbursed to eligible shareholders.

Cash dividends are often paid regularly (e.g., quarterly or annually), reflecting a company's financial health. Consistent payouts can enhance investor confidence and stabilize stock prices.

Stock Dividends

Stock dividends are distributions of additional shares to shareholders instead of cash. These dividends increase the number of shares owned proportionally but do not directly enhance shareholder wealth, as the value is diluted across more shares. Below is a structured breakdown of key aspects:

No.	Aspect	Details
1	**Type**	Additional shares of stock (not cash).
2	**Expression**	Percentage of existing shares (e.g., 10% stock dividend).
3	**Determination**	Based on company strategy, retained earnings, or desire to conserve cash.
4	**Frequency**	Less regular than cash dividends; varies by company needs.
5	**Benefits**	Conserves cash for reinvestment, signals long-term growth potential.
6	**Eligibility Requirement**	Shareholders must own the stock on the **record date** (same as cash dividends).
7	**Payment Date**	Date when additional shares are distributed to eligible shareholders.
8	**Impact on Shareholder Wealth**	No direct wealth increase; value dilutes as shares increase (e.g., 100 shares → 110 shares at reduced price).

No.	Aspect	Details
9	Investor Perception	Often viewed as less valuable than cash dividends, but may indicate confidence in future growth.

Stock dividends increase the total number of shares outstanding, diluting the price per share proportionally. For example, a 10% stock dividend for 100 shares grants 10 additional shares, but the market price adjusts downward to reflect the increased supply.

Dividend Reinvestment Plans (DRIPs)

Dividend Reinvestment Plans (DRIPs) allow shareholders to automatically reinvest cash dividends into additional shares of the company's stock. This method bypasses cash payouts, enabling passive, long-term growth through compounding. Below is a structured breakdown of key aspects:

No.	Aspect	Details
1	Type	Reinvestment of dividends into additional shares (no cash payout).
2	Mechanism	Cash dividends are used to purchase fractional or full shares automatically.
3	Enrollment Requirement	Shareholders must enroll via the company's transfer agent or brokerage.
4	Eligibility	Shareholders must own the stock by the **record date** (same as cash dividends).
5	Benefits	Enables compounding, passive growth, and potential discounted share prices (plan-dependent).
6	Frequency	Matches the dividend payout schedule (e.g., quarterly or annually).
7	Impact on Ownership	Increases total shares held over time without additional capital investment.
8	Considerations	May include fees or minimum investment requirements; terms vary by plan.

DRIPs eliminate the need for active portfolio management, as reinvested dividends purchase more shares automatically. Over time, this compounds returns, as new shares generate their own dividends.

To participate, shareholders must **enroll in the DRIP** and hold shares by the **record date**. Shares are typically purchased on the **payment date**, often at market price, though some plans offer discounts. While DRIPs reduce liquidity, they align with long-term wealth-building strategies by leveraging reinvestment and dollar-cost averaging.

Pros and Cons of Dividends

Dividends are a popular way for companies to distribute their profits to shareholders. While many investors see dividends as a sign of financial health and a source of income, there are also potential downsides to relying on dividend income. In this article, we'll take a closer look at the pros and cons of dividends, so you can make an informed decision about whether dividend-paying stocks are right for your investment portfolio.

Pros of Dividends	Cons of Dividends
Income Generation – Dividend-paying stocks provide a regular source of income, typically distributed quarterly or annually. This can be beneficial for retirees or investors seeking passive income.	**Limited Growth Potential** – Companies that pay dividends are usually well-established, meaning they may not offer the same rapid growth as high-growth or emerging companies.
Stability – Companies that consistently pay dividends are often financially stable and have strong earnings, making them attractive for conservative investors looking for lower-risk investments.	**Potential for Dividend Cuts** – Companies can reduce or eliminate dividends at any time, which can impact investors who rely on dividend income. Economic downturns or declining profits may lead to such cuts.
Long-Term Growth – Reinvesting dividends can lead to compounding growth over time, increasing overall returns and helping investors build wealth gradually.	**Price Volatility** – Stock prices may fluctuate due to dividend announcements. Prices may initially rise when a dividend is declared but could drop after the payout as investors sell off shares.
Tax Benefits – In many countries, dividends are taxed at a lower rate than capital gains or interest income, making them a tax-efficient way to earn investment income.	**Risk of Overvalued Stocks** – Some companies with high dividend yields may be overvalued, leading to potential stock price declines if market conditions shift. Investors need to assess valuations carefully.
Shareholder Value – Dividend payments signal financial strength and a company's	**Tax Implications** – Even though dividends may have lower tax rates, they are still subject to

Pros of Dividends	Cons of Dividends
commitment to returning profits to shareholders, which can attract more investors and boost stock demand.	taxation. Some companies may also withhold taxes before paying dividends, reducing investors' net earnings.

CHAPTER 15

Crypto currency

Cryptocurrency is a digital or virtual currency that uses cryptography for security and operates independently of a central bank. Cryptocurrencies use decentralized technology, such as blockchain, to create a transparent and secure digital ledger of all transactions. The most well-known and widely used cryptocurrency is Bitcoin, which was created in 2009.

Unlike traditional currencies, cryptocurrencies are not backed by any physical asset or government. Instead, their value is determined by supply and demand in the market. Cryptocurrencies can be exchanged for traditional currencies, goods, or services, and can be traded on various cryptocurrency exchanges.

One of the key features of cryptocurrencies is their decentralization, which means that they are not controlled by any government or institution. This makes them resistant to censorship, seizure, or manipulation by any single authority. Additionally, cryptocurrencies offer a high degree of privacy and anonymity in transactions.

However, cryptocurrencies are also associated with high volatility and risk. Their value can fluctuate widely in short periods, and they are not insured or backed by any government guarantee. Additionally, the lack of regulation and oversight has made cryptocurrencies susceptible to fraud, scams, and hacking attacks.

Despite these risks, cryptocurrencies have gained increasing popularity and adoption in recent years, as they offer a new form of digital asset and an alternative to traditional financial systems.

How Crypto currency Works

Cryptocurrencies utilize blockchain technology to function in a decentralized manner, negating the need for central authorities or intermediaries to verify transactions. This system is supported by a network of nodes, each responsible for maintaining copies of a digital ledger known as the blockchain.

Cryptocurrency Key Components

- **Cryptography** - Ensures secure digital transactions and authenticates users via digital signatures.
- **Blockchain** - A transparent, immutable ledger that records all transactions across a network of computers.
- **Mining** - The process of validating new transactions and recording them on the blockchain. Miners solve complex mathematical puzzles to achieve consensus and are rewarded with cryptocurrency for their efforts.
- **Wallets** - Digital tools that store private and public keys. Wallets facilitate the sending and receiving of cryptocurrencies and interact with various blockchains to enable users to monitor their balance.

Transaction Process Table:

Step	Action	Description
1	Transaction Initiation	Alice initiates a transaction to send Bitcoin to Bob, specifying the amount and Bob's wallet address.
2	Broadcast	The transaction is broadcasted to the network and waits in a pool of unconfirmed transactions.
3	Mining	Miners select the transaction from the pool and attempt to solve a cryptographic puzzle to validate it.
4	Confirmation	Upon solving the puzzle, the transaction is verified by the network and added to the blockchain.
5	Completion	Bob receives the Bitcoin in his wallet; the transaction is now secure and immutable.

Advantages and Challenges of Cryptocurrencies

While cryptocurrencies offer enhanced security, privacy, and the elimination of transaction fees typically associated with traditional banking, they also face scalability issues. These can result in slower transaction times and higher costs when the network is congested. Additionally, the value of cryptocurrencies can be highly volatile, and the lack of regulatory clarity poses risks and uncertainties.

Cryptocurrencies and blockchain technology provide a robust platform for secure and transparent financial transactions. They offer a decentralized alternative to traditional fiat currencies, promoting financial inclusion and efficiency. However, potential adopters should be aware of the risks associated with their use, including their volatility and evolving regulatory landscape.

Crypto Exchanges

Cryptocurrency exchanges are online platforms that allow users to buy, sell, and trade cryptocurrencies. They act as intermediaries between buyers and sellers, and offer a range of services, such as market data, trading tools, and security features.

To understand how cryptocurrency exchanges work, it's important to look at some key concepts, such as trading pairs, order books, liquidity, and security.

Trading pairs A trading pair is a pair of cryptocurrencies that can be traded against each other. For example, Bitcoin can be traded against Ethereum or USD can be traded against Bitcoin. Each trading pair has its own market, where buyers and sellers can place orders to buy or sell a certain amount of cryptocurrency at a certain price.

Order books An order book is a list of all the buy and sell orders for a particular trading pair. It shows the current price, the quantity of cryptocurrency being bought or sold, and the total value of the order. When a buyer and seller agree on a price, the order is executed, and the transaction is recorded on the blockchain.

Liquidity

Liquidity refers to the ability to buy or sell a cryptocurrency quickly and at a fair price. The more buyers and sellers there are on a particular exchange, the more liquid the market is, and the easier it is to buy and sell cryptocurrencies. Liquidity is important because it reduces the risk of price volatility and ensures that buyers and sellers can execute trades at a fair price.

Security

Security is a critical aspect of cryptocurrency exchanges, as they are often targeted by hackers and scammers. To ensure the security of their platform, exchanges use a range of measures, such as two-factor authentication, SSL encryption, and cold storage of funds. Cold storage is a method of storing cryptocurrency offline, which reduces the risk of theft or loss.

- Now that we understand these key concepts, let's look at how a typical cryptocurrency exchange works.
- Alice wants to buy some Bitcoin with USD.
- Alice opens an account on a cryptocurrency exchange and goes through the verification process.

- Alice deposits USD into her account on the exchange.
- Alice selects the BTC/USD trading pair and places a buy order for a certain amount of Bitcoin at a certain price.
- The order is added to the order book, and the exchange matches it with a sell order from another user who is selling Bitcoin at the same price.
- The order is executed, and the Bitcoin is transferred to Alice's exchange wallet.
- Alice can now withdraw the Bitcoin to her personal wallet, or use it for further transactions.
- This process is similar for selling Bitcoin or trading other cryptocurrencies, and the exchange earns a commission on each trade.

However, there are some challenges and risks associated with cryptocurrency exchanges. One of the biggest challenges is regulation, as many countries are still developing regulations for cryptocurrencies and exchanges. This can create uncertainty for users and limit the growth of the industry.

Additionally, exchanges are subject to security risks, such as hacking and fraud, which can result in the loss of funds. Users should be careful to choose reputable exchanges with strong security measures and should take steps to secure their own accounts and wallets.

Risks of Crypto currency

Cryptocurrency is a rapidly evolving and exciting field, with many potential benefits for users, including decentralization, security, and ease of use. However, like any new technology or asset class, it also comes with risks and challenges that users need to be aware of before investing or using cryptocurrencies. In this article, we will explore some of the risks associated with cryptocurrency and how users can mitigate them.

Volatility

One of the most significant risks associated with cryptocurrencies is volatility. Unlike traditional assets, such as stocks or bonds, the value of cryptocurrencies can fluctuate dramatically in a short period. This is due to a variety of factors, including market sentiment, regulatory changes, and technological advancements. Cryptocurrency users need to be aware of this risk and should consider diversifying their portfolio to minimize the impact of any individual asset's price movements.

Security

Cryptocurrency is digital, and the security of digital assets is always at risk of being compromised. Hackers can steal cryptocurrency, exploit vulnerabilities in exchanges, or attack blockchain networks. Users should be diligent in protecting their cryptocurrency, using secure storage methods such as hardware wallets or cold storage, and being cautious about sharing personal information or clicking on suspicious links.

Regulation

The regulatory landscape for cryptocurrencies is constantly evolving, with different countries taking different approaches to their treatment. This can create uncertainty for users and businesses and can affect the value of cryptocurrencies. Users need to stay up-to-date on the regulatory environment in their country and understand how changes may impact their holdings or transactions.

Liquidity

While many cryptocurrencies have significant market capitalizations, they may not always have the liquidity necessary to support large trades. This can lead to slippage, where the price of a cryptocurrency moves against the trader due to low liquidity. Additionally, low liquidity can create difficulties when buying or selling assets, which can lead to delays or increased transaction fees.

Scams and Fraud Cryptocurrencies have attracted scammers and fraudsters who take advantage of the unregulated nature of the market. Ponzi schemes, fake ICOs, and phishing attacks are common, and users need to be careful to avoid these scams. They should research projects and companies before investing, be cautious of unsolicited offers or messages, and avoid sharing private keys or personal information.

Adoption and Utility Finally, the adoption and utility of cryptocurrencies remain a significant risk. While the number of users and businesses accepting cryptocurrencies is growing, it remains a niche market with limited use cases in many parts of the world. The lack of adoption and utility can make cryptocurrencies challenging to use or sell, and can impact their value in the market.

To mitigate these risks, there are several steps users can take. Firstly, they should do their research and ensure they understand the risks and benefits of cryptocurrencies before investing or using them. Secondly, they should diversify their holdings and avoid investing all their capital in a single asset or market. Thirdly, they should use secure storage methods and follow best practices for digital security. Finally, they should stay informed of regulatory developments and news in the cryptocurrency industry to adapt to changing conditions.

CHAPTER 16

NFTs

Non-Fungible Tokens (NFTs) have emerged as one of the most talked-about developments in the digital asset space. NFTs represent a unique form of digital ownership that has the potential to revolutionize the way we think about digital assets. In this article, we will provide an introduction to NFTs and explore some of their key features, benefits, and use cases.

What are NFTs? NFTs are digital assets that represent ownership of a unique item, such as a piece of art, a collectible, or even a tweet. Unlike traditional cryptocurrencies like Bitcoin or Ethereum, which are fungible and can be exchanged for one another, each NFT is unique and cannot be replicated or exchanged for another asset. NFTs are typically created on a blockchain, which is a decentralized digital ledger that records all transactions and ownership information. The most common blockchain used for NFTs is Ethereum, which enables developers to create and trade NFTs using smart contracts.

How do NFTs work? NFTs are created using a process called "minting," which involves generating a unique digital asset and recording its ownership on a blockchain. This ownership is recorded using a smart contract, which is a self-executing computer program that controls the transfer of ownership between parties. Once an NFT is minted, it can be bought and sold on a marketplace or exchanged for other digital assets.

What are the benefits of NFTs? NFTs offer several benefits to creators, collectors, and investors, including:

- Authenticity: NFTs provide a way to prove ownership and authenticity of a digital asset, which is essential for creators and collectors of digital art, music, and other content.
- Traceability: The blockchain records all transactions and ownership information, providing a transparent and immutable record of the asset's ownership history.
- Liquidity: NFTs can be bought and sold on open marketplaces, providing a way for creators and investors to monetize their digital assets and for collectors to diversify their portfolios.

- Accessibility: NFTs provide a way for creators to reach a global audience and for collectors to access unique digital assets from around the world.

What are the use cases for NFTs? NFTs have a wide range of use cases across industries, including art, music, gaming, and sports. Some of the most popular use cases include:

Digital Art: NFTs provide a new way for artists to monetize their digital creations, as they can sell their art directly to collectors on open marketplaces. This has led to a surge in interest in digital art, with several high-profile sales, such as the $69 million sale of Beeple's "Everydays: The First 5000 Days" at Christie's auction house in March 2021.

Music: NFTs offer a new way for musicians to monetize their music and engage with their fans. Musicians can sell unique digital collectibles, such as album covers or concert tickets, or provide exclusive access to behind-the-scenes content or VIP experiences.

Gaming: NFTs have the potential to revolutionize the gaming industry, as they can provide a way to monetize in-game assets and create unique collectibles that can be traded on open marketplaces. This has led to the emergence of "play-to-earn" games, where players can earn cryptocurrencies or NFTs by playing the game.

Sports: NFTs offer a new way for sports teams and athletes to engage with their fans and monetize their brand. Athletes can sell digital collectibles, such as autographed photos or game-worn jerseys, or provide exclusive access to VIP experiences or events.

What are the challenges of NFTs?

Associated with NFTs, there are also several challenges that need to be addressed before they can become more widely adopted. Some of the key challenges include:

Environmental Impact: One of the main concerns with NFTs is their environmental impact. The process of minting an NFT requires a significant amount of energy, as it involves complex calculations on a blockchain network. This energy consumption can lead to a significant carbon footprint, which is a concern for many individuals and organizations.

Scalability: The current infrastructure of blockchain networks like Ethereum is not designed to handle the high volumes of transactions that are needed for NFTs to be used on a large scale. This can lead to slow transaction times and high fees, which can deter users from buying and selling NFTs.

Regulation: The regulatory landscape for NFTs is still in its early stages, and it is unclear how these assets will be regulated in the future. This uncertainty can lead to a lack of trust among potential users and investors.

Market Saturation: As the popularity of NFTs continues to grow, there is a risk of market saturation, where the market becomes flooded with low-quality or irrelevant NFTs. This can lead to a decline in demand for NFTs and a loss of value for those who have invested in them.

Lack of Interoperability: NFTs are currently limited to specific blockchain networks, which can create barriers to entry for new users and limit the potential uses for these assets. There is a need for greater interoperability between different blockchain networks to enable NFTs to be used in a wider range of applications.

Custody and Security: NFTs are digital assets that are stored on a blockchain network, which can make them vulnerable to theft or hacking. There is a need for secure custody solutions and protocols to ensure that NFTs are protected from unauthorized access or theft.

NFTs represent a new form of digital ownership that has the potential to revolutionize the way we think about digital assets. They offer a range of benefits, including authenticity, traceability, liquidity, and accessibility, and have a wide range of use cases across industries. However, there are also several challenges that need to be addressed before NFTs can become more widely adopted, including environmental impact, scalability, regulation, market saturation, lack of interoperability, and custody and security. As the market for NFTs continues to evolve, it will be important to address these challenges to ensure that NFTs can realize their full potential.

How NFTs Work

NFTs, or non-fungible tokens, are unique digital assets that are stored on a blockchain network. Unlike fungible tokens like Bitcoin or other cryptocurrencies, which are interchangeable and have the same value, NFTs are one-of-a-kind and have their own distinct value. NFTs can be used to represent a wide range of digital assets, including artwork, music, video games, virtual real estate, and more.

Here's a step-by-step breakdown of how NFTs work:

Creation: The process of creating an NFT starts with the creation of a digital asset, which can be in the form of an image, video, or other digital file. The creator then "mints" the NFT by uploading the file to a blockchain network, along with information about the asset, such as its name, description, and unique identifier.

Blockchain Verification: The blockchain network verifies the authenticity and ownership of the NFT through a process called "smart contracts." These contracts are self-executing programs that enforce the rules and conditions of the transaction, such as ownership rights and transferability.

Ownership and Transfer: Once the NFT is minted and verified, it is owned by the creator or whoever they choose to sell it to. The ownership of the NFT is recorded on the blockchain network, which allows for transparent tracking and transferability of the asset. NFTs can be bought and sold on various online marketplaces, where users can bid on them or purchase them directly.

Proof of Authenticity: NFTs provide proof of authenticity and ownership for digital assets, which can be a major advantage for artists and creators. This is because it allows them to prove that they are the original creators of the asset and ensures that they receive proper compensation for their work.

Royalties: One of the unique features of NFTs is that they can be programmed to automatically pay royalties to the creator each time the asset is resold on a secondary market. This allows creators to benefit from the increasing value of their work and can create a sustainable revenue stream for them.

Storage and Access: NFTs are stored on a blockchain network, which provides a secure and decentralized way to store digital assets. Users can access their NFTs through digital wallets, which allow them to view and transfer their assets.

Overall, NFTs are a unique and innovative way to represent and transfer ownership of digital assets. They provide a range of benefits, including proof of authenticity, transparent tracking and transferability, and the ability to pay royalties to creators. However, as with any new technology, there are also several challenges that need to be addressed, such as scalability, environmental impact, regulation, and security.

NFT Marketplaces

NFTs, or non-fungible tokens, have become increasingly popular in recent years as a new way to represent and transfer ownership of digital assets. NFT marketplaces are online platforms where users can buy, sell, and trade these unique digital assets. These marketplaces are a critical component of the NFT ecosystem, as they provide a centralized platform for users to discover and purchase NFTs.

OpenSea

OpenSea is currently the largest NFT marketplace, with over 4 million items and 135,000 users. It offers a wide range of NFTs, including art, music, domain names, virtual real estate, and more. OpenSea is a decentralized marketplace that operates on the Ethereum blockchain, and it has a user-friendly interface that allows users to easily search and filter for specific types of NFTs.

One of the unique features of OpenSea is that it allows users to create their own NFTs without any coding knowledge. This makes it an accessible platform for both creators and collectors.

Additionally, OpenSea provides a set of APIs that developers can use to build their own applications and tools on top of the platform.

Rarible

Rarible is another popular NFT marketplace that operates on the Ethereum blockchain. It allows users to buy, sell, and create their own NFTs, and it has a user-friendly interface that makes it easy to navigate. Rarible offers a range of NFTs, including art, collectibles, memes, and more.

One of the unique features of Rarible is that it allows creators to customize the royalty rate that they receive each time their NFT is resold on the secondary market. This provides creators with a sustainable revenue stream and helps to support the development of their work.

SuperRare

SuperRare is a curated NFT marketplace that focuses on high-quality digital art. It operates on the Ethereum blockchain and has a strict curation process that ensures that all NFTs listed on the platform are of the highest quality. SuperRare offers a range of features, including auctions, bidding, and social features that allow collectors and creators to interact with each other.

One of the unique features of SuperRare is that it provides a social verification process that allows users to verify their identity and reputation on the platform. This helps to build trust between buyers and sellers and ensures that high-quality work is showcased on the platform.

Nifty Gateway

Nifty Gateway is an NFT marketplace that focuses on digital art and collectibles. It operates on the Ethereum blockchain and has a user-friendly interface that makes it easy for users to buy, sell, and trade NFTs. Nifty Gateway offers a range of features, including timed releases, auctions, and limited edition drops.

One of the unique features of Nifty Gateway is that it collaborates with high-profile artists and brands to release exclusive NFT collections. This has helped to attract a wider audience to the platform and has increased the visibility of NFTs as a new asset class.

Foundation

Foundation is an NFT marketplace that focuses on digital art and design. It operates on the Ethereum blockchain and has a curation process that ensures that all NFTs listed on the platform are of the highest quality. Foundation offers a range of features, including auctions, bidding, and social features that allow collectors and creators to interact with each other.

One of the unique features of Foundation is that it allows creators to set a reserve price for their NFTs, which helps to ensure that they receive a fair price for their work. Additionally,

Foundation has a focus on sustainability, and it uses carbon offsets to neutralize the carbon footprint of the transactions that take place on the platform.

KnownOrigin

KnownOrigin is an NFT marketplace that focuses on digital art. It operates on the Ethereum blockchain and has a curation process that ensures that all NFTs listed on the platform are of the highest quality. KnownOrigin offers a range of features, including auctions, bidding, and social features that allow collectors and creators to interact with each other.

One of the unique features of KnownOrigin is that it allows creators to donate a portion of their sales to charity. This has helped to attract socially conscious collectors to the platform and has increased the visibility of NFTs as a new way to support charitable causes.

MakersPlace

MakersPlace is an NFT marketplace that focuses on digital art. It operates on the Ethereum blockchain and has a curation process that ensures that all NFTs listed on the platform are of the highest quality. MakersPlace offers a range of features, including timed releases, auctions, and social features that allow collectors and creators to interact with each other.

One of the unique features of MakersPlace is that it uses a process called "content unlocking" to ensure that the NFTs listed on the platform are unique and cannot be replicated. This involves encrypting the original digital asset and providing the buyer with a decryption key that unlocks the NFT.

Async Art

Async Art is an NFT marketplace that focuses on programmable art. It operates on the Ethereum blockchain and allows creators to create dynamic and interactive art that can be modified and updated over time. Async Art offers a range of features, including auctions, bidding, and social features that allow collectors and creators to interact with each other.

One of the unique features of Async Art is that it allows creators to add "layers" to their artwork that can be controlled by the buyer. This means that the buyer can customize and modify the artwork over time, creating a unique and dynamic piece of digital art.

NFT marketplaces are a critical component of the NFT ecosystem, providing a centralized platform for users to discover and purchase unique digital assets. The top NFT marketplaces offer a range of features, including auctions, bidding, and social features that allow collectors and creators to interact with each other. They also use a range of strategies to ensure that the NFTs listed on the platform are of the highest quality, including curation processes, social verification, and content unlocking. As the popularity of NFTs continues to grow, these marketplaces will play an increasingly important role in the NFT ecosystem, helping to facilitate the transfer of ownership and providing a platform for creators to monetize their digital assets.

Risks of NFTs

Non-fungible tokens (NFTs) have captured the attention of both creators and collectors, offering innovative opportunities in digital ownership and art. However, the excitement around NFTs is tempered by significant risks due to their novel nature.

The NFT marketplace operates without much regulatory oversight, leaving participants vulnerable to fraud and disputes with limited recourse. The authenticity of NFTs can be challenging to verify, and without standardized regulations, resolving conflicts becomes more complicated.

Another concern is the extreme volatility in NFT values, driven more by fluctuating market demands than inherent value. This unpredictability can lead to substantial price swings, influenced by a small number of transactions or notable events within the NFT community.

The market for NFTs also suffers from liquidity issues. The niche appeal and subjective value of NFTs can make them difficult to sell quickly without significant price concessions. This lack of liquidity can frustrate both potential sellers looking to realize gains and buyers seeking specific items.

From a cybersecurity perspective, while blockchain—the underlying technology for NFTs—is secure, risks still loom. Users' private keys, essential for accessing and transferring NFTs, if stolen or lost, can lead to irrevocable losses. Furthermore, vulnerabilities in NFT platforms have been exploited by cybercriminals, leading to theft and fraud.

Legally, the NFT realm presents uncharted territory. The application of traditional copyright and intellectual property laws to NFTs remains unclear, creating potential legal challenges for creators and collectors alike.

Environmental impact is another critical issue. The significant energy and computing power required to create and trade NFTs contribute to considerable carbon emissions, raising sustainability concerns among critics.

Lastly, NFTs are not immune to social and ethical dilemmas. They can exacerbate economic disparities, potentially serve as tools for money laundering, and impact traditional arts and culture sectors in unforeseeable ways.

Despite these concerns, NFTs continue to grow in popularity, drawing interest across various sectors. It's essential for participants to navigate these risks carefully, considering both the innovative potentials and the significant challenges of engaging with NFTs.

Risk Factor	Impact
Regulatory Uncertainty	Lack of legal frameworks leading to disputes and challenges in rights enforcement
Market Volatility	Rapid, unpredictable fluctuations in value
Liquidity Issues	Difficulty in buying/selling NFTs at desired prices
Cybersecurity Threats	Potential for theft or loss due to compromised security measures
Legal Ambiguity	Unclear application of existing laws to NFT transactions
Environmental Impact	High energy consumption raising sustainability concerns
Social & Ethical	Potential to magnify economic inequality and facilitate illicit activities

Market analysis

Conducting a market analysis is a critical first step for any business considering expansion. It offers insights into the current market dynamics, customer preferences, and overall industry movements, all of which are crucial for making informed decisions about growth strategies.

Understanding Your Target Market Getting a clear picture of your potential customers is vital. This process involves analyzing demographic data such as age, gender, income levels, and location. Beyond demographics, understanding psychographics—like customer values, interests, and lifestyles—helps tailor your approach to meet specific needs and wants. Knowing who your customers are and what they seek ensures that your expansion efforts are aligned with their expectations.

Competitor Analysis Gaining a competitive edge requires a thorough understanding of your rivals. This step involves identifying who your main competitors are, assessing their strengths and weaknesses, and understanding their product offerings and pricing strategies. By doing so, you can pinpoint gaps in the market and areas where your business can stand out. This analysis helps in formulating strategies to differentiate your products or services, potentially capturing a larger market share.

Industry Trends Staying updated with industry trends is crucial for sustaining growth and innovation. This includes technological advancements, regulatory changes, and shifts in consumer behavior. Being aware of these trends can aid in anticipating market needs and adapting your business model accordingly. For instance, if there is a growing trend towards sustainability in your industry, you might consider incorporating eco-friendly practices or products to attract a broader customer base.

A comprehensive market analysis not only aids in identifying expansion opportunities but also minimizes risks associated with entering new markets or introducing new products. By thoroughly understanding the market, competitors, and industry trends, a business can develop a robust strategy that maximizes chances of success and ensures long-term sustainability.

Financial planning

Effective financial planning is vital when considering expanding your business. It ensures that the expansion is not only viable but also positions the business for sustained growth. Here's a streamlined approach to crafting a robust financial plan:

Creating a Comprehensive Budget The first step in financial planning is to develop a detailed budget that accounts for all the foreseeable expenses related to the expansion. This includes direct costs like marketing, additional personnel, new equipment, and facility upgrades. A well-thought-out budget helps in assessing the financial viability of the expansion plans and identifies opportunities for cost optimization.

Forecasting Revenue Estimating future revenues is critical, especially when expanding. This forecast should be based on a mix of historical sales data, industry benchmarks, and market analysis to estimate the revenue increase from expanding your market reach or product line. Accurate revenue forecasting aids in setting realistic financial goals and expectations for the growth phase.

Estimating Expenses Alongside revenue forecasting, it's crucial to project the expenses that will accrue due to expansion. This involves a detailed analysis of costs related to new hires, marketing campaigns, technology upgrades, and any other operational expenses that will increase as a result of scaling up. Understanding these costs upfront will help in maintaining financial balance and ensuring the expansion doesn't strain your existing resources.

Identifying Funding Sources Expansion often requires external funding. It's important to explore and identify suitable funding sources that align with your business goals. These could include traditional bank loans, venture capital, angel investors, or government grants. Each funding source comes with its own set of advantages and considerations like interest rates, equity dilution, or stringent repayment terms. Choosing the right mix of financing options can significantly impact the long-term financial health of your business.

Focusing on these essential elements, businesses can develop a financial plan that not only supports their expansion objectives but also enhances overall financial stability and growth potential. This plan acts as a roadmap, guiding businesses through the complexities of expansion while ensuring financial discipline and foresight.

Staffing

When expanding a business, ensuring you have the right team in place is crucial for the success and sustainability of the growth. Careful planning in staffing will help manage this transition smoothly.

Understanding Staffing Needs

The first step is to evaluate the specific needs of your expanding business. This includes identifying how many new employees are required and the specific roles they will fill. Consider the skills and expertise that are essential for these roles and how they fit into your current organizational structure. This assessment helps in creating roles that complement the existing workforce and contribute effectively to the business's expansion goals.

Crafting Detailed Job Descriptions

Once the roles are clearly defined, the next step is crafting precise job descriptions. These should outline not only the duties and responsibilities of each position but also the skills and qualifications required. Well-articulated job descriptions are instrumental in attracting the right talent pool. They serve as a primary communication tool that sets clear expectations for potential candidates about what the job entails and what the company expects from them.

Recruitment Process

With the job descriptions in hand, the recruitment process begins. This involves sourcing candidates through various channels, screening applications, conducting interviews, and performing reference checks. The goal is to find candidates who not only have the required professional qualifications but also align with the company culture and values. This fit is crucial for long-term employee retention and satisfaction.

Onboarding and Training

Hiring the right candidates is just the beginning. Properly integrating them into your company through a structured onboarding process is vital. This includes training new employees not only on their specific job roles but also on the company's policies, culture, and goals. Effective onboarding and ongoing development opportunities ensure that employees are engaged and have the necessary tools to succeed in their new roles.

Focusing on these aspects, businesses can enhance their workforce effectively to support expansion. The aim is not just to fill positions but to build a team that will drive the company's growth forward. This strategic approach to staffing will contribute significantly to the successful scaling of the business.

Marketing and sales strategies for business growth

Marketing and sales strategies are pivotal in steering business growth, directly influencing how successfully a business can penetrate new markets, boost its revenue, and outpace competitors. Crafting a robust marketing and sales plan enables businesses to engage new customers effectively and leverage these interactions into long-term relationships and increased sales.

Targeted Marketing Techniques

Effective marketing often hinges on the ability to deliver customized messages to a well-defined audience. Targeted marketing enhances customer interaction and fosters deeper connections by addressing specific needs and preferences. Employing persona-based marketing is an excellent strategy. This technique involves developing detailed customer profiles based on varied attributes like demographics and behavior, allowing for more nuanced and persuasive communications.

Segmentation is another crucial strategy, grouping customers by shared characteristics such as age or income to tailor communications effectively. Personalization ramps up this customization by leveraging data like browsing and purchase histories to craft individualized experiences, thereby increasing the relevance and impact of marketing efforts.

Content Marketing Approaches

Content marketing is essential for drawing in and engaging potential customers by offering them valuable content. This strategy not only boosts brand visibility but also establishes a business's authority in its field, encouraging more robust customer engagement.

Blogging stands out as a highly effective content marketing tactic. Regular posts about relevant topics not only enrich customer knowledge but also bolster the business's credibility as an industry thought leader. Social media marketing amplifies this effect by providing a platform to share content widely and engage directly with customers, enhancing brand visibility and fostering community.

Video marketing, too, plays a critical role in today's digital marketing strategies. Videos can effectively showcase a business's products or services and highlight company culture, making content not only more engaging but also shareable, thus extending the brand's reach.

Expanding Marketing and Sales Reach

Beyond these strategies, exploring new sales channels can dramatically enhance market reach and customer base. E-commerce platforms, for example, provide a global audience and a streamlined path from marketing to sales. Additionally, partnering with influencers or other brands can open up new customer segments and add credibility to the brand.

Continuous Improvement and Adaptation

The marketing and sales landscape is ever-evolving, necessitated by changes in consumer behavior and technological advancements. It's crucial for businesses to stay adaptive and continuously refine their strategies based on real-time data analytics and customer feedback. This not only helps in optimizing marketing efforts but also ensures that the sales strategies are aligned with the latest market dynamics.

Implementing these comprehensive marketing and sales strategies can significantly aid businesses in navigating competitive markets, fostering customer loyalty, and driving sustainable growth.

Search Engine Optimization (SEO)

Search engine optimization (SEO) is essential for any business looking to boost online visibility and attract more traffic to its website. SEO involves tweaking various aspects of a site — from its content and structure to its technical setup — to rank higher on search engine results pages.

Starting with keyword research is crucial. This step identifies relevant, high-traffic keywords potential customers are using to find products or services similar to those the business offers. Integrating these keywords throughout the website helps enhance visibility and improve search rankings.

Optimizing on-page elements is another key strategy. This includes refining the content and layout of the website, such as improving titles, meta descriptions, headers, and images to make them more relevant and appealing to both search engines and users. Ensuring the content not only includes keywords but also provides value to readers is vital for engaging visitors and encouraging longer site interactions.

Building backlinks from other reputable websites is a powerful off-page optimization strategy. These links function as a form of endorsement, enhancing the site's perceived trustworthiness and boosting its search engine rankings.

Technical SEO should not be overlooked, as it involves optimizing the website's backend elements like site speed and mobile-friendliness. These adjustments ensure a smoother, more engaging user experience, which search engines favor when ranking sites.

Local SEO is critical for businesses targeting specific geographic areas. It focuses on tailoring the site's content and SEO strategies to include local keywords and regional specifics, which helps attract a local audience.

Moreover, integrating SEO with content marketing efforts can significantly enhance a site's visibility. Producing quality content such as informative articles, engaging videos, and graphics encourages other websites to link back to the site, further strengthening its SEO.

SEO requires ongoing effort and adaptation. Regularly analyzing the site's performance, adjusting strategies based on analytics, and keeping abreast of search engine algorithm updates are essential for maintaining and improving search rankings.

Carefully applying these SEO strategies, businesses can significantly increase their online presence, attract more visitors, and foster continuous growth.

Sales Strategies

Sales strategies are crucial for any business aiming to enhance revenue and expand its customer base. They focus on identifying potential customers, convincing them to purchase products or services, and fostering enduring relationships.

Optimizing the sales funnel is a vital strategy. This process guides potential customers from initial awareness through to interest, decision-making, purchase, and eventually, loyalty. Enhancing the sales funnel improves conversion rates at every stage, boosting sales and revenue.

Customer relationship management (CRM) is another pivotal strategy, utilizing data to enhance customer relationships. By tracking interactions, preferences, and behaviors, businesses can better understand and cater to customer needs, which enhances loyalty and encourages repeat business.

Developing the sales team is also essential. A skilled and motivated sales team can significantly increase the effectiveness of sales efforts, resulting in higher sales and revenue.

Referral marketing is a potent growth strategy that leverages existing customers to attract new ones. Incentivizing customers to refer others can be an efficient and cost-effective marketing approach.

Implementing a customer referral program offers rewards to customers who bring in new business. This could be through discounts, free products or services, or other exclusive perks.

Affiliate marketing expands reach by partnering with other businesses or influencers who promote the business's offerings. Offering a commission or referral fee to these affiliates helps tap into a broader potential customer base.

Using social proof is another effective method. Showcasing positive reviews, testimonials, and endorsements from satisfied customers can attract new ones by building trust and credibility.

Together, these strategies not only aim to increase sales but also to build a sustainable customer base by continuously engaging and satisfying the needs of the market.

Legal and regulatory considerations for expanding a business

Expanding a business requires careful consideration of various legal and regulatory requirements to avoid potential legal liabilities, fines, and other obstacles that could impede growth. One critical aspect is business entity formation, which involves selecting the appropriate structure, such as a sole proprietorship, partnership, limited liability company (LLC), or corporation. The choice of entity affects tax liabilities, exposure to personal liability, and the company's management organization.

As a business grows, it may need to acquire additional licenses and permits, which vary based on industry and location. These can include local business licenses, zoning permits, environmental permits, and professional licenses. Neglecting to secure the necessary permissions can lead to legal issues and financial penalties.

With expansion often comes the need to hire more staff, requiring compliance with various employment laws. These include regulations related to anti-discrimination, wages, hours, and workplace safety. Non-compliance can lead to lawsuits, financial penalties, and reputational damage. Protecting intellectual property is paramount for businesses creating unique products or content. This includes securing trademarks, patents, copyrights, and safeguarding trade secrets to prevent infringement issues and protect the business's brand and reputation.

Business expansion typically involves new contracts with customers, suppliers, and partners. It's important to ensure these contracts are well-drafted to protect the business's interests and comply with applicable laws. Disputes over contracts can be expensive and distract from core business operations, so legal advice is often necessary. Business growth can also change a company's tax obligations, necessitating compliance with local, state, and federal tax laws, including those governing income, sales, and payroll taxes. Inadequate compliance can trigger financial penalties and legal challenges.

Handling sensitive customer data requires adherence to data privacy and security laws, such as the General Data Protection Regulation (GDPR) or the California Consumer Privacy Act (CCPA). Violations can lead to severe penalties and damage to the business's reputation.

Expanding internationally introduces complexity, requiring adherence to international trade and export control laws, like the Foreign Corrupt Practices Act (FCPA) and the International Traffic in Arms Regulations (ITAR). Non-compliance can result in severe legal repercussions and harm to the company's global standing.

These considerations underscore the importance of a meticulous approach to legal and regulatory compliance during business expansion.

CHAPTER 17

Taxation and Accounting

Taxation is an important consideration for businesses of all sizes and industries. Business taxes can be a significant expense and impact the profitability of the company. Understanding the tax landscape and obligations for businesses is critical for planning and compliance. This article will provide an overview of taxation for businesses, including the types of business taxes, tax rates, and key considerations for businesses.

Types of Business Taxes

There are several types of business taxes that companies may be required to pay, depending on their legal structure and industry. The most common types of business taxes include:

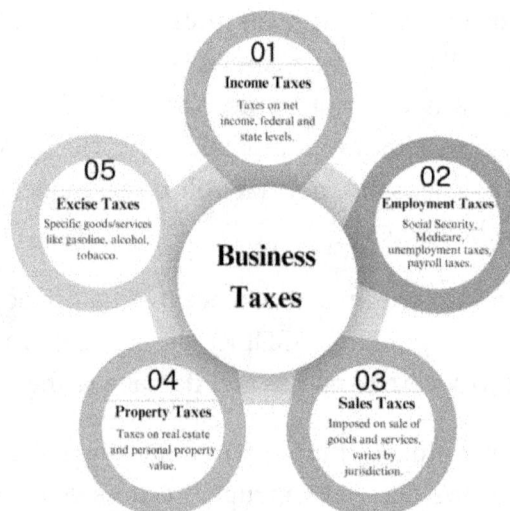

Income Taxes: Business income taxes are taxes on the net income earned by a business during a given tax year. The federal government, as well as most states, impose income taxes on businesses. The tax rate varies based on the amount of taxable income earned by the business.

Employment Taxes: Employment taxes include Social Security and Medicare taxes, federal and state unemployment taxes, and other payroll taxes. These taxes are typically paid by employers and are based on the wages paid to employees.

Sales Taxes: Sales taxes are imposed by state and local governments on the sale of goods and services. The tax rate varies based on the jurisdiction, and businesses are required to collect and remit sales tax to the appropriate authorities.

Property Taxes: Property taxes are taxes on the value of real estate and personal property. Businesses that own real property or personal property are subject to property taxes at the local and state levels.

Excise Taxes: Excise taxes are taxes on specific goods or services, such as gasoline, alcohol, and tobacco products. The tax rate varies based on the type of product or service and is typically included in the price paid by the consumer.

Tax Rates

The tax rates for businesses vary based on the type of tax and the level of government imposing the tax. Federal income tax rates for corporations are currently set at a flat rate of 21%. However, individual taxpayers who own a small business that is not a separate legal entity, such as a sole proprietorship or partnership, report business income on their personal tax returns and are taxed at their individual tax rate. State income tax rates vary widely and are typically based on the amount of taxable income earned by the business within the state.

Employment tax rates vary based on the type of tax and the employee's earnings. The Social Security tax rate is currently 12.4% of an employee's wages, with half of the tax paid by the employer and half by the employee. The Medicare tax rate is currently 2.9%, with the employer and employee each paying 1.45%. Employers are also required to pay federal and state unemployment taxes based on the wages paid to employees.

Sales tax rates vary based on the jurisdiction and the type of product or service. In some states, the sales tax rate is uniform across the state, while in other states, the rate varies by county or city. Some states also have exemptions or reduced rates for certain products or services.

Property tax rates vary based on the value of the property and the local tax rate. Businesses that own real property or personal property are subject to property taxes at the local and state levels.

Excise tax rates vary based on the type of product or service. For example, the federal excise tax rate on gasoline is currently 18.4 cents per gallon, while the excise tax rate on tobacco products is based on the type of product and the amount sold.

Tax planning and compliance

Tax planning and compliance are important considerations for businesses of all sizes and industries. Effective tax planning can help businesses minimize their tax liability, while compliance ensures that businesses meet their tax obligations and avoid penalties and fines. This article will provide an overview of tax planning and compliance, including key considerations and strategies for businesses.

Tax Planning

Tax planning involves the process of analyzing a business's financial situation to minimize its tax liability. The goal of tax planning is to legally reduce the amount of taxes a business owes, while maximizing its profits. Effective tax planning requires a thorough understanding of the tax code, as well as the business's financial situation and objectives.

There are several tax planning strategies that businesses can use to minimize their tax liability:

Maximize Deductions: Businesses should take advantage of all available deductions to reduce their taxable income. Deductions can include expenses related to operations, such as rent, salaries, and supplies.

Accelerate Expenses: Businesses can accelerate certain expenses, such as equipment purchases, to take advantage of the depreciation deduction. By accelerating these expenses, businesses can reduce their taxable income and lower their tax liability.

Delay Income: Businesses can delay income to the following tax year to reduce their taxable income for the current year. By delaying income, businesses can defer their tax liability to a later date.

Invest in Retirement Accounts: Businesses can invest in retirement accounts, such as a 401(k) or IRA, to reduce their taxable income. Contributions to retirement accounts are tax-deductible and can reduce a business's tax liability.

Take Advantage of Tax Credits: Businesses can take advantage of tax credits to reduce their tax liability. Tax credits are available for certain expenses, such as research and development, energy efficiency, and employee training.

Consider Entity Structure: The legal structure of a business can impact its tax liability. For example, a business that operates as a sole proprietorship or partnership is taxed at the individual tax rate, while a business that operates as a corporation is taxed at the corporate tax rate. By choosing the right legal structure, businesses can minimize their tax liability.

Tax Compliance

Tax compliance involves the process of meeting a business's tax obligations, including filing tax returns and paying taxes on time. Non-compliance can result in penalties, fines, and legal action. Effective tax compliance requires a thorough understanding of the tax code, as well as the business's tax obligations and deadlines.

There are several key considerations for businesses to ensure tax compliance:

- Keep Accurate Records: Businesses should keep accurate records of all income and expenses, including receipts and invoices. Records should be kept for at least three years.
- Know Tax Obligations: Businesses should be aware of their tax obligations, including filing deadlines and payment due dates. Businesses should also be aware of any tax credits or deductions they may be eligible for.
- File Timely Tax Returns: Businesses should file their tax returns on time to avoid penalties and fines. In some cases, businesses may be required to file tax returns quarterly or annually.
- Pay Taxes on Time: Businesses should pay their taxes on time to avoid penalties and interest charges. Payments can be made electronically or by mail.
- Monitor Tax Law Changes: Tax laws and regulations can change frequently. Businesses should stay up-to-date on changes to the tax code to ensure compliance.
- Work with Tax Professionals: Businesses may benefit from working with tax professionals, such as accountants or tax attorneys, to ensure compliance and minimize their tax liability.

Accounting principles and practices

Accounting is an essential function of any business, regardless of its size or industry. The goal of accounting is to accurately record and report a business's financial transactions and performance. Accounting principles and practices provide a framework for businesses to follow when recording financial information, preparing financial statements, and making financial decisions. This article will provide an overview of accounting principles and practices, including key considerations and strategies for businesses.

Accounting Principles

There are several accounting principles that businesses should follow to ensure the accuracy and integrity of their financial information:

- ❖ Accrual Accounting: Accrual accounting involves recording transactions when they occur, not when cash is exchanged. This provides a more accurate picture of a business's financial performance over time.

- ❖ Consistency: Businesses should use consistent accounting methods and practices when recording financial transactions. This ensures that financial information is comparable over time and across different businesses.
- ❖ Materiality: Businesses should only record and report financial information that is material, or significant, to the business's financial performance. This helps to ensure that financial information is relevant and useful to stakeholders.
- ❖ Conservatism: The conservatism principle requires businesses to be cautious when reporting financial information. This means that businesses should not overstate assets or revenue, and should be conservative when estimating future expenses.
- ❖ Cost Principle: The cost principle requires businesses to record assets at their original cost, not their market value. This provides a more accurate picture of a business's financial position and performance.
- ❖ Full Disclosure: The full disclosure principle requires businesses to provide all relevant and necessary financial information to stakeholders. This includes footnotes and disclosures in financial statements.

Accounting Practices

There are several accounting practices that businesses should follow to ensure the accuracy and integrity of their financial information:

- ❖ Record Transactions: Businesses should record all financial transactions in a systematic and organized manner. This includes recording all revenue, expenses, and other financial transactions in a timely manner.
- ❖ Reconcile Accounts: Businesses should reconcile their bank and credit card accounts on a regular basis to ensure that all transactions are accurately recorded.
- ❖ Prepare Financial Statements: Businesses should prepare accurate and timely financial statements, including balance sheets, income statements, and cash flow statements.
- ❖ Analyze Financial Data: Businesses should analyze their financial data to identify trends and patterns, and to make informed financial decisions.
- ❖ Budgeting and Forecasting: Businesses should develop and use budgets and forecasts to plan and manage their financial performance. This helps businesses to identify potential issues and opportunities, and to make informed financial decisions.

Internal Controls: Businesses should implement internal controls to ensure the accuracy and integrity of their financial information. This includes procedures and policies for recording and reporting financial transactions, as well as for protecting and securing financial information.

Auditing and financial reporting

Auditing and financial reporting are two important components of a business's financial management system. Auditing is the process of examining a company's financial records, statements, and transactions to ensure accuracy and compliance with accounting standards and regulatory requirements. Financial reporting, on the other hand, involves preparing and presenting a company's financial statements to shareholders, investors, and other stakeholders. In this article, we will discuss the importance of auditing and financial reporting, key considerations for businesses, and best practices for effective financial management.

Importance of Auditing

Auditing plays a critical role in ensuring the accuracy and reliability of a company's financial records and reports. It provides an objective evaluation of a company's financial performance and can help identify potential errors or fraud. Auditing is also important in ensuring compliance with legal and regulatory requirements, such as the Sarbanes-Oxley Act of 2002, which requires public companies to establish and maintain effective internal controls over financial reporting.

Key Considerations for Auditing

There are several key considerations that businesses should keep in mind when conducting an audit:

- ❖ Independence: Auditors should be independent and objective, free from conflicts of interest or bias. This ensures that their evaluation is fair and impartial.
- ❖ Compliance: Auditors should ensure that the company's financial statements are in compliance with accounting standards and regulatory requirements. This includes verifying that all financial information is accurate and complete.
- ❖ Materiality: Auditors should focus on material items, or items that have a significant impact on the company's financial performance. This helps to ensure that the audit is focused on the most important areas of the business.
- ❖ Documentation: Auditors should document their findings and conclusions, providing a clear and detailed record of the audit process.

Best Practices for Effective Auditing

To ensure an effective audit, businesses should follow best practices such as:

- ❖ Establishing Internal Controls: Businesses should establish effective internal controls, including policies and procedures for financial reporting, to ensure the accuracy and integrity of their financial records.
- ❖ Hiring Qualified Auditors: Businesses should hire qualified auditors who have the necessary skills, experience, and expertise to conduct a thorough and effective audit.
- ❖ Conducting Regular Audits: Businesses should conduct regular audits to ensure ongoing compliance with accounting standards and regulatory requirements.
- ❖ Following Audit Recommendations: Businesses should follow the recommendations of auditors to address any issues or deficiencies identified during the audit.

Financial Reporting

Financial reporting is the process of preparing and presenting a company's financial statements, which provide information about the company's financial performance and position. The financial statements include the balance sheet, income statement, and cash flow statement.

Key Considerations for Financial Reporting

There are several key considerations that businesses should keep in mind when preparing their financial statements:

- ❖ Accuracy: Financial statements should accurately reflect the company's financial position and performance, including all relevant financial information.
- ❖ Consistency: Financial statements should be consistent over time, allowing stakeholders to compare performance from one period to another.
- ❖ Compliance: Financial statements should be in compliance with accounting standards and regulatory requirements.
- ❖ Transparency: Financial statements should be transparent, providing stakeholders with clear and meaningful information about the company's financial performance.

Best Practices for Effective Financial Reporting

To ensure effective financial reporting, businesses should follow best practices such as:

- ❖ Maintaining Accurate Records: Businesses should maintain accurate and complete financial records, ensuring that all financial transactions are recorded in a timely and accurate manner.
- ❖ Hiring Qualified Professionals: Businesses should hire qualified professionals, such as certified public accountants (CPAs), to prepare and review their financial statements.
- ❖ Using Accounting Software: Businesses should use accounting software to streamline financial reporting and ensure the accuracy and consistency of financial information.
- ❖ Conducting Regular Reviews: Businesses should conduct regular reviews of their financial statements to ensure accuracy

CHAPTER 18

Risk Management

Risk management is the process of identifying, assessing, and mitigating potential risks that could negatively impact an organization's objectives. It is a critical function of any organization, as risks can arise from a variety of sources, including financial, operational, legal, reputational, and strategic risks.

The goal of risk management is to proactively identify and manage risks in a way that minimizes the impact of those risks on an organization's operations, finances, and reputation. Effective risk management can help an organization to avoid or minimize potential losses, maintain its operations, and achieve its goals.

The Risk Management Process

The risk management process typically involves the following steps:

Risk Identification: This involves identifying potential risks that could impact an organization's objectives. Risks can arise from a variety of sources, including operational, financial, legal, reputational, and strategic risks.

Risk Assessment: Once potential risks have been identified, the next step is to assess the likelihood and potential impact of each risk. This involves evaluating the probability of the risk occurring, as well as the potential financial and non-financial impact of the risk.

Risk Mitigation: After potential risks have been identified and assessed, the next step is to develop and implement strategies to mitigate those risks. This could involve implementing policies and procedures, investing in technology or infrastructure, or purchasing insurance to transfer risk.

Monitoring and Review: The final step in the risk management process is to continuously monitor and review the effectiveness of the risk management strategies that have been implemented. This allows organizations to identify new risks as they emerge and adjust their risk management strategies as needed.

Types of Risk

In the field of risk management, there are many different types of risk that organizations may face. These risks can be broadly categorized into several different categories based on the nature of the risk, its potential impact, and the strategies that can be used to mitigate it. In this article, we will discuss some of the most common types of risk that organizations may encounter, including financial risk, operational risk, reputational risk, strategic risk, and compliance risk.

Financial Risk

Financial risk is a type of risk that relates to an organization's financial health, including its ability to generate revenue, meet financial obligations, and manage financial resources. Financial risks can take many forms, including market risk, credit risk, liquidity risk, and currency risk.

Market risk refers to the risk that an organization's investments or assets will decrease in value due to changes in market conditions or external events, such as changes in interest rates, inflation, or economic growth. Market risk can be managed through a variety of strategies, including diversification, hedging, and portfolio optimization.

Credit risk refers to the risk that an organization will experience financial losses due to the failure of a borrower to repay a loan or fulfill other financial obligations. Credit risk can be managed through credit analysis, risk-based pricing, and collateral requirements.

Liquidity risk refers to the risk that an organization will be unable to meet its financial obligations due to a lack of cash or other liquid assets. Liquidity risk can be managed through cash flow management, short-term borrowing, and access to credit facilities.

Currency risk refers to the risk that an organization's financial performance will be impacted by changes in exchange rates. Currency risk can be managed through currency hedging strategies, such as forward contracts, options, and swaps.

Operational Risk

Operational risk is a type of risk that relates to an organization's ability to effectively execute its operational processes and procedures. Operational risks can arise from a variety of sources, including human error, system failures, process inefficiencies, and external events.

Human error is a common source of operational risk, and can include mistakes made by employees, inadequate training, or poor communication. System failures, such as software or hardware failures, can also lead to operational risk.

Process inefficiencies can also create operational risk, as poorly designed or executed processes can lead to delays, errors, or other problems. External events, such as natural disasters, supply chain disruptions, or regulatory changes, can also create operational risk.

Operational risk can be managed through a variety of strategies, including process improvement, automation, training, and contingency planning.

Reputational Risk

Reputational risk is a type of risk that relates to an organization's reputation or public image. Reputational risk can arise from a variety of sources, including negative publicity, product recalls, ethical lapses, or other issues that can damage an organization's reputation.

Reputational risk can have a significant impact on an organization's finances and operations, as it can lead to decreased sales, loss of customers, or legal and regulatory action. Reputational risk can be managed through proactive reputation management, effective crisis communication, and a strong culture of ethics and compliance.

Strategic Risk

Strategic risk is a type of risk that relates to an organization's strategic objectives and the potential impact of external events on those objectives. Strategic risk can arise from a variety of sources, including changes in market conditions, shifts in consumer behavior, or disruptive technologies.

Strategic risk can have a significant impact on an organization's long-term performance, as it can impact the ability to achieve strategic goals and objectives. Strategic risk can be managed through effective strategic planning, scenario analysis, and monitoring of external trends and developments.

Compliance Risk

Compliance risk is a type of risk that relates to an organization's compliance with legal and regulatory requirements. Compliance risk can arise from a variety of sources, including failure to comply with laws, regulations, and industry standards, as well as ethical lapses and misconduct.

Non-compliance with legal and regulatory requirements can result in significant financial and reputational losses, as well as legal and regulatory action, including fines, penalties, and sanctions. Compliance risk can be managed through effective compliance programs, training, monitoring, and reporting.

Environmental, Social, and Governance (ESG) Risk

Environmental, Social, and Governance (ESG) risk is a type of risk that relates to an organization's impact on the environment, society, and the economy. ESG risk can arise from a variety of sources, including climate change, human rights violations, corruption, and other ethical and social issues.

ESG risk can have a significant impact on an organization's financial performance, as investors and other stakeholders increasingly consider ESG factors when making investment decisions. ESG risk can be managed through effective sustainability programs, ethical and responsible business practices, and proactive stakeholder engagement.

Cybersecurity Risk

Cybersecurity risk is a type of risk that relates to an organization's exposure to cyber threats, including unauthorized access, theft of data, and disruption of systems and networks. Cybersecurity risk can arise from a variety of sources, including malicious actors, human error, and vulnerabilities in software and hardware.

Cybersecurity risk can have a significant impact on an organization's operations, finances, and reputation, as well as the privacy and security of sensitive information. Cybersecurity risk can be managed through effective cybersecurity programs, training, risk assessments, and incident response planning.

Risk Management Techniques

Risk management is the process of identifying, assessing, and managing risks in order to minimize potential losses and maximize opportunities. There are many different techniques that organizations can use to manage risk, depending on their specific needs and goals. In this article, we will explore some of the most common risk management techniques and how they can be used to mitigate risk.

Risk Avoidance

Risk avoidance is a risk management technique that involves completely avoiding activities, processes, or situations that pose a potential risk. This technique is typically used when the potential consequences of a risk are too severe or when the cost of managing the risk outweighs the potential benefits.

> *For example, an organization may choose to avoid investing in a particular industry or market that is known to be highly volatile or risky. This may help to protect the organization from potential losses, but it also means that they may miss out on potential gains.*

Risk Reduction

Risk reduction is a risk management technique that involves taking steps to reduce the likelihood or impact of a potential risk. This technique is often used when the potential consequences of a risk are significant, but the benefits of the activity or process outweigh the potential costs.

> *For example, an organization may implement a cybersecurity program to reduce the likelihood of a cyber attack or invest in diversifying their portfolio to reduce their exposure to market risk. These steps may help to reduce the impact of potential risks, but they may not completely eliminate them.*

Risk Transfer

Risk transfer is a risk management technique that involves transferring the financial consequences of a potential risk to another party. This technique is typically used when the potential consequences of a risk are too severe or when the cost of managing the risk is too high.

> *For example, an organization may purchase insurance to transfer the financial consequences of a potential risk, such as property damage or liability claims, to an insurance company. This can help to reduce the organization's exposure to potential losses, but it also means that they will pay a premium for the insurance coverage.*

Risk Acceptance

Risk acceptance is a risk management technique that involves accepting the potential consequences of a risk without taking any specific action to manage it. This technique is often used when the potential consequences of a risk are relatively minor or when the cost of managing the risk outweighs the potential benefits.

> *For example, an organization may choose to accept the risk of losing a small amount of money on a low-risk investment, rather than investing in a more risky but potentially more profitable opportunity. This may help to protect the organization from potential losses, but it also means that they may miss out on potential gains.*

Risk Sharing

Risk sharing is a risk management technique that involves sharing the financial consequences of a potential risk with another party. This technique is typically used when the potential consequences of a risk are too severe for one party to bear alone.

> *For example, an organization may enter into a joint venture with another organization to share the financial and operational risks associated with a particular project or investment. This can help to reduce the organization's exposure to potential losses, but it also means that they will share any potential profits with the other party.*

Risk Mitigation

Risk mitigation is a risk management technique that involves taking proactive steps to identify and reduce the impact of potential risks. This technique is often used when the potential consequences of a risk are significant, but the benefits of the activity or process outweigh the potential costs.

> *For example, an organization may implement risk management procedures and controls to reduce the likelihood and impact of fraud or other financial risks. This can help to reduce the organization's exposure to potential losses and protect their finances and reputation.*

Contingency Planning

Contingency planning is a risk management technique that involves developing a plan to respond to potential risks if they occur. This technique is often used when the potential consequences of a risk are significant and may require a specific course of action to address them.

> *For example, an organization may develop a contingency plan for a natural disaster or other unexpected event that could impact their operations. The plan would outline specific steps to take in the event of a disaster, such as evacuating personnel, securing facilities, and communicating with stakeholders.*

Scenario Planning

Scenario planning is a risk management technique that involves developing and analyzing different potential scenarios to identify potential risks and develop contingency plans. This technique is often used when the potential consequences of a risk are difficult to predict or when there are many variables that could impact the outcome.

> *For example, an organization may develop scenarios for different market conditions or economic situations in order to identify potential risks and opportunities. This can help the organization to make more informed decisions and develop contingency plans for a range of potential outcomes.*

Business Continuity Planning

Business continuity planning is a risk management technique that involves developing a plan to ensure that critical business operations can continue in the event of a disruption or disaster. This technique is often used when the potential consequences of a risk could disrupt or impact critical business processes.

> *For example, an organization may develop a business continuity plan to ensure that critical systems and processes can continue to function in the event of a cyber attack or other disruption. The plan would outline specific steps to take to restore operations and minimize potential losses.*

Monitoring and Review

Monitoring and review is a risk management technique that involves ongoing monitoring and analysis of potential risks and the effectiveness of risk management strategies. This technique is important for ensuring that risk management strategies remain effective and relevant as conditions and circumstances change.

> *For example, an organization may regularly review and update their risk management procedures and controls to ensure that they are effective in addressing potential risks. This may involve conducting regular risk assessments, reviewing incident reports, and soliciting feedback from stakeholders.*

Risk Assessment

Risk assessment is a fundamental component of effective risk management. It involves the process of identifying and analyzing potential risks to an organization, evaluating their likelihood and impact, and developing strategies to address them. By conducting risk assessments, organizations can gain a better understanding of their exposure to risks and develop targeted risk management plans to mitigate potential losses.

The following are the key steps involved in conducting a risk assessment:

Identify Potential Risks

The first step in conducting a risk assessment is to identify potential risks that could impact the organization. Risks can come from a variety of sources, including financial, operational, legal, regulatory, and reputational factors. To identify potential risks, organizations can conduct a review of internal and external data sources, such as financial statements, incident reports, customer complaints, and industry reports.

Analyze Risks

Once potential risks have been identified, the next step is to analyze them in terms of their likelihood and impact. This involves assessing the likelihood of a risk occurring and the potential impact it could have on the organization. Organizations can use various techniques, such as risk matrices or qualitative risk analysis, to assess and prioritize risks.

Develop Risk Management Strategies

Based on the results of the risk analysis, organizations can develop risk management strategies to address the identified risks. Risk management strategies may involve implementing controls to prevent or mitigate potential risks, transferring risk to a third party through insurance or contractual arrangements, or accepting the risk and developing contingency plans to minimize potential losses.

Implement Risk Management Strategies

Once risk management strategies have been developed, the next step is to implement them. This may involve implementing new policies, procedures, or controls to mitigate potential risks, or communicating risk management plans to relevant stakeholders.

Finally, it is important to regularly monitor and review risk management strategies to ensure that they remain effective and relevant over time. This may involve conducting periodic risk assessments, reviewing incident reports, or soliciting feedback from stakeholders.

Benefits of Risk Assessment

Conducting a risk assessment offers several benefits to organizations, including:

By conducting a risk assessment, organizations can gain a better understanding of their exposure to potential risks and develop targeted risk management plans to mitigate them. This can help to improve risk awareness across the organization and ensure that all stakeholders are aware of potential risks.

By identifying and addressing potential risks, organizations can minimize the potential for losses and disruptions to their operations. This can help to protect the organization's finances, reputation, and stakeholders.

By using a risk-based approach to decision making, organizations can make more informed and effective decisions that take into account potential risks and their potential impact. This can help to improve decision making across the organization and ensure that risks are considered in all business decisions.

Many regulatory frameworks require organizations to conduct risk assessments and implement appropriate risk management strategies. By conducting regular risk assessments, organizations can ensure that they remain compliant with relevant regulations and standards.

Challenges of Risk Assessment

While risk assessment offers many benefits to organizations, it can also present several challenges, including:

Conducting a comprehensive risk assessment requires access to a wide range of data sources, including financial data, incident reports, and industry reports. Ensuring the quality and availability of this data can be a challenge, particularly for smaller organizations with limited resources.

Risk assessment can be a complex process, particularly for larger organizations with multiple business units and operations. Ensuring that all potential risks are identified and addressed can be a challenge, and may require input from a range of stakeholders.

The process of assessing the likelihood and impact of potential risks can be subjective and may be influenced by individual perspectives and biases.

Conducting a comprehensive risk assessment can be a costly process, particularly for larger organizations with complex operations. The cost of implementing risk management strategies can also be significant, particularly if significant changes to operations or infrastructure are required.

Risk assessment involves predicting the likelihood and impact of potential risks, which can be subject to a high degree of uncertainty. This uncertainty can make it challenging to develop accurate risk management plans, particularly for emerging risks or those that are difficult to quantify.

Implementing risk management strategies may require significant changes to operations, policies, and procedures. This can lead to resistance from stakeholders who may be reluctant to change established ways of doing business. Overcoming this resistance may require effective communication and stakeholder engagement strategies.

CHAPTER 19

Corporate Finance

Corporate finance is a field that deals with the financial management of businesses and corporations. It involves the management of financial resources, including the procurement and allocation of funds to optimize business operations and increase the value of the company. Corporate finance is concerned with decision-making regarding investment, financing, and dividend policies that are aimed at maximizing shareholder value.

The primary goal of corporate finance is to maximize shareholder value by managing financial resources efficiently. To achieve this goal, corporate finance involves a wide range of financial management activities, including financial planning and analysis, investment analysis, capital budgeting, risk management, and financial reporting.

Capital Budgeting

Capital budgeting is a process that involves analyzing potential investments in order to determine their financial viability and potential return on investment. The goal of capital budgeting is to allocate financial resources to investments that will generate the highest return on investment while minimizing risk. Capital budgeting is a critical component of corporate finance and is essential for the long-term success of any business.

Capital budgeting involves several steps, including identifying potential investment opportunities, estimating future cash flows, evaluating the risks associated with the investment, determining the appropriate discount rate, and calculating the net present value (NPV) of the investment. The NPV is a measure of the expected return on investment and is used to determine whether an investment is financially viable.

Types of Investment Opportunities

There are several types of investment opportunities that businesses may consider when engaging in capital budgeting. These may include:

- Expansion Projects: These are projects that involve expanding the business by increasing production capacity, adding new product lines, or opening new locations.
- Replacement Projects: These are projects that involve replacing existing assets, such as machinery or equipment, with newer, more efficient models.
- Research and Development Projects: These are projects that involve the development of new products, services, or technologies.
- Marketing and Advertising Projects: These are projects that involve investing in marketing and advertising campaigns to increase brand awareness and drive sales.

Estimating Future Cash Flows

One of the key components of capital budgeting is estimating future cash flows. This involves forecasting the cash inflows and outflows associated with the investment over its useful life. Cash inflows may include revenues generated by the investment, while cash outflows may include costs associated with the investment, such as capital expenditures and operating expenses.

Estimating future cash flows can be a challenging process, as it involves predicting future economic conditions, market trends, and consumer behavior. In order to generate accurate cash flow estimates, businesses must consider a wide range of factors, including historical financial data, industry trends, and macroeconomic factors.

Another important component of capital budgeting is evaluating risk. All investments involve a certain level of risk, and it is important for businesses to assess the risks associated with an investment before committing resources. Risks associated with an investment may include market risks, such as changes in demand for the product or service, operational risks, such as production issues or supply chain disruptions, and financial risks, such as changes in interest rates or currency fluctuations.

The discount rate is a critical component of the capital budgeting process, as it is used to calculate the NPV of the investment. The discount rate represents the cost of capital and is used to discount future cash flows to their present value. The appropriate discount rate depends on several factors, including the risk associated with the investment, the cost of borrowing, and the company's cost of equity.

Calculating the Net Present Value

The net present value (NPV) is a measure of the expected return on investment and is used to determine whether an investment is financially viable. The NPV is calculated by subtracting the initial investment from the present value of the expected cash flows. A positive NPV indicates that the investment is expected to generate a return that exceeds the cost of capital, while a negative NPV indicates that the investment is not financially viable.

Working Capital Management

Working capital management is a crucial aspect of corporate finance that deals with managing a company's short-term financial obligations, such as paying suppliers, managing inventory, and meeting operational expenses. Efficient working capital management is essential to maintain a company's liquidity, cash flow, and profitability. In this article, we will explore what working capital management is, its components, and how companies can optimize their working capital.

What is Working Capital Management?

Working capital management is a set of strategies and processes that companies use to manage their short-term financial obligations and assets. It involves ensuring that the company has enough liquid assets to meet its current obligations while still maintaining enough funds to pursue growth opportunities.

Working capital management includes managing cash, inventory, accounts payable, and accounts receivable. Cash management involves managing the company's cash flows, ensuring that it has enough cash to pay its short-term obligations. Inventory management involves ensuring that the company has enough stock to meet customer demand while minimizing inventory holding costs. Accounts payable management involves managing the company's outstanding bills and ensuring timely payment to suppliers. Accounts receivable management involves managing the company's outstanding customer invoices and ensuring timely receipt of payments.

Components of Working Capital Management

The following are the key components of working capital management:

Cash Management: Cash management involves managing the company's cash inflows and outflows. The goal is to ensure that the company has enough cash to meet its short-term obligations while optimizing cash balances to earn the highest possible return.

Inventory Management: Inventory management involves managing the company's stock levels to meet customer demand while minimizing inventory holding costs. The goal is to maintain the right level of inventory to meet customer demand while minimizing the cost of holding inventory.

Accounts Payable Management: Accounts payable management involves managing the company's outstanding bills and ensuring timely payment to suppliers. The goal is to manage the company's cash flow by delaying payments to suppliers while still maintaining good relationships with them.

Accounts Receivable Management: Accounts receivable management involves managing the company's outstanding customer invoices and ensuring timely receipt of payments. The goal is to manage the company's cash flow by collecting payments from customers as quickly as possible while still maintaining good customer relationships.

Optimizing Working Capital

Optimizing working capital involves finding the right balance between short-term obligations and short-term assets. This requires a careful analysis of a company's cash flow, inventory, accounts payable, and accounts receivable. The following are some strategies that companies can use to optimize their working capital:

Improving Cash Flow: Companies can improve their cash flow by accelerating cash inflows and delaying cash outflows. This can be done by offering discounts to customers for early payments, negotiating better payment terms with suppliers, and reducing inventory holding costs.

Reducing Inventory: Companies can reduce inventory by improving demand forecasting, adopting lean manufacturing practices, and using just-in-time inventory management.

Managing Accounts Payable: Companies can manage accounts payable by negotiating better payment terms with suppliers, taking advantage of early payment discounts, and using electronic invoicing and payment systems.

Managing Accounts Receivable: Companies can manage accounts receivable by offering early payment discounts, using electronic invoicing and payment systems, and actively pursuing overdue payments.

Capital Structure

Capital structure refers to the mix of financing sources that a company uses to fund its operations and growth. This includes debt and equity financing, as well as any hybrid securities that combine features of both debt and equity. Capital structure decisions can have a significant impact on a company's financial performance and value, and thus are an important consideration for corporate finance.

In general, there are two main types of financing: debt financing and equity financing. Debt financing involves borrowing money from lenders, who are then repaid with interest over time.

Equity financing involves selling ownership shares in the company, giving investors a stake in the business in exchange for their investment.

Determining the optimal capital structure for a company is a complex decision that depends on a variety of factors, including the company's industry, stage of development, risk profile, and cost of capital. The cost of capital refers to the total cost of financing for a company, including both the cost of debt and the cost of equity.

Debt financing is generally less expensive than equity financing, since lenders typically charge lower interest rates than equity investors demand in returns. However, debt financing comes with the risk of default, meaning the company is unable to repay the debt, which can lead to bankruptcy. Debt financing can also limit the company's financial flexibility, since lenders may require collateral or impose restrictions on the use of funds.

Equity financing, on the other hand, does not require repayment and does not impose restrictions on the use of funds. However, equity financing is generally more expensive than debt financing, since investors require a higher rate of return to compensate for the higher risk of investing in an ownership stake rather than lending money. Equity financing can also dilute existing shareholders' ownership stakes in the company, as new shares are issued to investors.

To determine the optimal capital structure for a company, corporate finance professionals use a variety of techniques and metrics, including weighted average cost of capital (WACC), net present value (NPV), internal rate of return (IRR), and other financial models. These models take into account a variety of factors, including the cost of different types of financing, the expected return on investment, and the risks associated with each financing option.

One common approach to capital structure is to target a certain debt-to-equity ratio, which is the proportion of the company's total financing that comes from debt versus equity. The optimal debt-to-equity ratio depends on a variety of factors, including the company's risk profile, cost of capital, and industry norms.

Other considerations in capital structure include the timing and frequency of debt and equity issuances, the types of debt and equity securities used, and the impact of financing decisions on shareholder value. In general, companies with strong cash flows and low levels of debt may be more likely to use debt financing to take advantage of the lower cost of capital, while companies with high growth potential may be more likely to use equity financing to avoid taking on too much debt and limiting their financial flexibility.

Capital structure decisions are an important part of corporate finance, and can have a significant impact on a company's financial performance and value. By carefully considering the costs and benefits of different types of financing, companies can make informed decisions that help them achieve their strategic goals and maximize shareholder value.

CHAPTER 20

Financial Planning

Financial planning is the process of setting and achieving personal or organizational financial goals by creating a comprehensive strategy to manage finances and achieve long-term objectives. The financial planning process is aimed at optimizing financial resources to help individuals or organizations achieve financial independence, stability, and security.

Effective financial planning involves analyzing and understanding the financial position, identifying financial goals, and developing a plan of action to achieve those goals. The process should also include regular evaluation and adjustment to ensure the plan remains relevant to changing circumstances and economic conditions.

The key steps in the financial planning process include:

Assessment of Current Financial Position - The first step in financial planning is to assess the current financial position. This involves gathering information about income, expenses, assets, and liabilities. This will help to establish the current financial status and identify any gaps that need to be addressed.

Setting Financial Goals - After assessing the current financial position, the next step is to set financial goals. Financial goals can be short-term, medium-term, or long-term. Examples of financial goals include building an emergency fund, buying a house, saving for a child's education, or planning for retirement.

Developing a Financial Plan - The third step is to develop a comprehensive financial plan that outlines the steps needed to achieve financial goals. The financial plan should consider income, expenses, assets, and liabilities, as well as economic factors such as inflation, interest rates, and market performance.

Implementing the Financial Plan - The fourth step is to implement the financial plan. This involves taking the necessary steps to achieve the financial goals outlined in the plan. This could include reducing expenses, increasing income, investing in assets, and paying down debt.

Monitoring and Reviewing the Financial Plan - The final step in the financial planning process is to monitor and review the financial plan regularly. This is important to ensure that the plan remains relevant and effective, and to make adjustments as needed to ensure that financial goals are being achieved.

Financial planning can encompass a wide range of areas, including budgeting, saving, investing, retirement planning, estate planning, and risk management. Each of these areas plays an important role in achieving financial goals and ensuring long-term financial security.

Budgeting is a key component of financial planning, as it helps to manage cash flow and control expenses. A budget is a financial plan that outlines expected income and expenses over a specified period. A budget can be used to identify areas where expenses can be reduced, as well as areas where additional income may be needed.

Saving is another important aspect of financial planning, as it helps to build wealth over time. Saving can be used to build an emergency fund, save for short-term goals, or invest in long-term assets such as retirement accounts or real estate.

Investing is a critical component of financial planning, as it helps to build wealth over the long-term. Investments can include stocks, bonds, mutual funds, real estate, and other assets. The selection of investments will depend on factors such as risk tolerance, investment goals, and time horizon.

Retirement planning is a key aspect of financial planning, as it involves saving and investing for retirement. Retirement planning can include strategies such as 401(k) plans, Individual Retirement Accounts (IRAs), and other retirement savings vehicles.

Estate planning is an important aspect of financial planning, as it involves planning for the transfer of assets and property after death. Estate planning can include strategies such as wills, trusts, and other legal instruments.

Risk management is also an important aspect of financial planning, as it involves identifying and managing risks that could negatively impact financial goals. This could include risks such as job loss, disability, illness, or death.

Importance of Financial Planning

Financial planning is the process of creating a comprehensive roadmap that outlines an individual or organization's financial goals and strategies to achieve them. It involves assessing the current financial situation, identifying short-term and long-term goals, and developing an action plan to reach those goals. In this article, we will explore the importance of financial planning and the benefits it provides to individuals and organizations.

The primary objective of financial planning is to help individuals and organizations achieve their financial goals. By setting realistic financial goals, individuals can better understand the steps required to achieve them. Financial planning takes into account various factors such as income, expenses, assets, and liabilities to determine how much money can be allocated towards achieving those goals. A well-crafted financial plan provides a clear roadmap that helps individuals and organizations prioritize their spending, manage their debt, and invest their money in a way that aligns with their objectives.

Financial planning involves analyzing an individual or organization's financial situation in detail. It involves assessing the current financial position, including cash flow, assets, liabilities, income, and expenses. This assessment helps in identifying the strengths and weaknesses in the financial position and helps in making informed decisions about future investments and financial strategies. By having a clear picture of the current financial position, individuals and organizations can better understand their capacity to take on additional debt, make investments, and identify areas where expenses can be reduced.

Debt management is a crucial component of financial planning. A well-designed financial plan considers all the existing debts, their interest rates, and repayment schedules. This assessment enables individuals and organizations to identify the most effective ways to manage their debt. With a clear understanding of their financial position and the impact of different types of debt, individuals and organizations can choose the most suitable debt management strategies. These strategies may include consolidation of high-interest debt, negotiating with creditors to reduce interest rates, and making extra payments towards high-interest debts.

One of the primary benefits of financial planning is that it enables individuals and organizations to make better financial decisions. By analyzing the current financial position, identifying goals, and creating a comprehensive action plan, individuals and organizations can make more informed decisions about how to invest their money, manage their debt, and reduce expenses. A well-crafted financial plan can help individuals and organizations make smarter financial decisions that align with their goals and objectives.

A well-designed financial plan can help individuals and organizations build wealth over time. By identifying their goals, analyzing their current financial position, and developing a comprehensive action plan, individuals and organizations can make informed decisions about how to invest their money. This may include investing in stocks, bonds, mutual funds, real estate, or other types of investments. A solid financial plan takes into account the risk profile of the individual or organization and balances the desire for growth with the need for stability.

Risk management is an essential component of financial planning. A well-crafted financial plan takes into account various risks, including market risk, inflation risk, interest rate risk, and longevity risk. By identifying these risks, individuals and organizations can develop strategies to mitigate them. This may include diversifying investments, investing in insurance products, or building an emergency fund to manage unforeseen circumstances. A solid financial plan considers all the risks and develops strategies to manage them effectively.

Steps in Financial Planning

Financial planning is the process of assessing one's financial situation, setting goals, and creating a plan to achieve those goals. It involves understanding your current financial situation, setting achievable goals, and taking the necessary steps to achieve those goals. Financial planning can help individuals and organizations to make informed financial decisions and can assist them in achieving their financial objectives. In this article, we will discuss the steps involved in financial planning.

Step 1: Set financial goals

The first step in financial planning is to identify your financial goals. This could include goals such as saving for retirement, buying a home, paying off debt, or funding a child's education. Once you have identified your goals, you can start to create a plan to achieve them.

Step 2: Assess your current financial situation

The second step in financial planning is to assess your current financial situation. This includes analyzing your income, expenses, assets, and liabilities. By understanding your current financial situation, you can develop a plan that takes into account your financial strengths and weaknesses.

Step 3: Develop a budget

Once you have assessed your current financial situation, you can create a budget. A budget is a plan that outlines your income and expenses, and helps you to manage your money effectively. A budget can help you to identify areas where you can cut costs and save money, as well as areas where you may need to allocate more funds.

Step 4: Develop a savings plan

Saving is an essential part of financial planning. Once you have developed a budget, you can create a savings plan. This involves setting aside a portion of your income each month to achieve your financial goals. You can use different savings vehicles, such as a savings account, a retirement account, or a brokerage account.

Step 5: Develop an investment plan

Investing is another essential part of financial planning. Once you have developed a savings plan, you can create an investment plan. An investment plan involves selecting investments that align with your financial goals, risk tolerance, and time horizon. Investments can include stocks, bonds, mutual funds, and exchange-traded funds (ETFs).

Step 6: Develop a debt management plan

Managing debt is also an important part of financial planning. If you have outstanding debts, you should develop a debt management plan. This involves identifying your debts, prioritizing them based on interest rates, and developing a plan to pay them off. You may also want to consider consolidating your debts to simplify the repayment process.

Step 7: Review and adjust your plan

Financial planning is an ongoing process. It's important to review your plan regularly and make adjustments as necessary. This may involve revising your budget, changing your savings or investment plan, or adjusting your debt management plan. By regularly reviewing and adjusting your plan, you can ensure that it remains relevant and effective.

Benefits of Financial Planning

Financial planning is the process of assessing an individual's financial goals and creating a roadmap to achieve those goals. It involves analyzing one's financial situation, creating a budget, developing a plan for saving and investing, and monitoring progress towards the goals. Financial planning has many benefits that can help individuals achieve their financial goals and lead a secure and stress-free life.

One of the main benefits of financial planning is that it provides clarity and focus on financial goals. By setting specific and measurable goals, individuals can develop a plan to achieve those goals. It helps individuals to prioritize their financial decisions and allocate resources more effectively to achieve their financial objectives.

Financial planning provides a framework for making informed financial decisions. It helps individuals to assess the risks and returns associated with different investment options and choose the most appropriate ones based on their goals, risk tolerance, and time horizon. It also helps individuals to avoid impulsive or emotional financial decisions that can lead to negative consequences.

Financial planning helps individuals to manage their cash flow more effectively. By creating a budget and tracking their expenses, individuals can identify areas where they are overspending and make adjustments to their spending habits. This can help individuals to reduce their debt, increase their savings, and achieve their financial goals faster.

Financial planning also involves assessing and managing the risks associated with different financial decisions. It helps individuals to protect their assets and reduce the impact of unforeseen events such as illness, job loss, or economic downturns. Through insurance policies and other risk management strategies, individuals can mitigate the financial impact of these events and safeguard their financial well-being.

Effective tax planning is an important part of financial planning. It helps individuals to minimize their tax liabilities and maximize their after-tax returns. By understanding the tax implications of different financial decisions, individuals can make informed decisions that can lead to significant tax savings over time.

Financial planning can help individuals to increase their savings and accumulate wealth over time. By creating a plan to save and invest regularly, individuals can benefit from compounding returns and achieve their financial goals faster. Financial planning also helps individuals to identify opportunities to increase their income and reduce their expenses, which can further increase their savings and wealth accumulation.

Effective financial planning can also lead to an improved standard of living. By achieving financial goals such as homeownership, retirement, or education, individuals can enjoy greater financial security and a more comfortable lifestyle. Financial planning also helps individuals to reduce financial stress and improve their overall well-being.

CHAPTER 21

Human Capital Management & Organizational Culture

Human capital management and organizational culture are pivotal in steering a company towards success. This section delves into the importance of viewing employees as vital assets that significantly boost performance. It covers creating inclusive workplace cultures that support diversity, encourage open communication, and promote teamwork. The text also explores effective leadership development and the maintenance of ethical labor practices, which together enhance productivity and ensure compliance with regulations. By focusing on a comprehensive approach to workforce management, this discussion equips business leaders with essential strategies to cultivate a productive and sustainable work environment.

The Role of Human Capital in Business Success

Human capital is fundamentally the collective abilities, knowledge, and skills that employees possess, which contribute significantly to the overall value and operational capacity of a business. It represents a form of wealth that can be directed towards the achievement of organizational goals and is central to the sustainability and growth of any company.

At its core, the concept of human capital revolves around the idea that employees are not just replaceable resources but are central to the competitive advantage of a business. Investing in human capital means providing training, education, and development opportunities to employees, which equips them with new skills and knowledge. This investment enhances their productivity and efficiency, leading to better business outcomes.

For instance, a company that invests in leadership training for its managers can expect improvements in team performance and morale, which often translate into increased productivity and reduced turnover. Likewise, offering employees opportunities for professional development not only expands their skill sets but also boosts their engagement and loyalty to the company. Engaged employees are more likely to go above and beyond in their roles, contributing to innovation and the overall success of the business.

Moreover, the role of human capital extends beyond just the individual contributions of employees. It also encompasses creating a culture that values continuous learning and improvement. A culture that supports and encourages professional growth attracts talented individuals who are looking for workplaces that will help them thrive. This attraction is especially crucial in industries where competition for highly skilled workers is intense.

The impact of human capital on business success is also evident in how it influences organizational culture. Companies that actively develop and manage their human capital tend to foster a positive workplace culture. This culture is characterized by mutual respect, a shared vision, and aligned goals. When employees feel that their growth is integral to the company's strategy, it enhances their sense of belonging and purpose, which can lead to higher job satisfaction and productivity.

However, managing human capital effectively requires understanding and addressing the diverse needs of employees. This involves not only skill development but also creating an inclusive environment that respects and utilizes the diverse backgrounds and perspectives of all employees. Diversity in the workforce can spark creativity and innovation, providing fresh insights and solutions that a more homogenous workforce might overlook.

Furthermore, as the global business environment becomes increasingly complex, the need for a well-rounded and adaptable workforce becomes more critical. Businesses that can leverage their human capital to quickly respond to changes and challenges will be better positioned to succeed. This agility is partly derived from having employees who are well-trained, highly motivated, and capable of thinking critically.

The role of human capital in business success is multifaceted and profound. From enhancing individual employee performance to shaping a positive organizational culture, the benefits of investing in human resources are extensive. As businesses continue to navigate a rapidly changing world, the strategic management of human capital will remain a key determinant of long-term success. Companies that recognize and act on the potential of their human capital are more likely to achieve sustainable growth and maintain a competitive edge in their respective industries.

Building Inclusive Workplace Cultures

Creating an inclusive workplace culture is essential for fostering a positive and productive work environment. When employees feel valued, respected, and included, they are more likely to be engaged, motivated, and committed to their work. An inclusive workplace embraces diversity in all its forms, including differences in race, gender, age, background, abilities, and perspectives. Companies that prioritize inclusivity benefit from increased innovation, improved employee satisfaction, and stronger business performance.

A truly inclusive workplace starts with leadership. Leaders play a crucial role in setting the tone for an organization's culture. When executives and managers actively promote inclusivity, it sends a clear message that diversity and equal opportunities are valued. Inclusive leadership means creating policies and practices that support all employees, listening to diverse voices, and addressing biases that may exist in the workplace. Training programs that focus on cultural awareness and unconscious bias help leaders and employees recognize and eliminate barriers to inclusion.

Recruitment and hiring practices also play a significant role in building an inclusive workplace. Companies that prioritize diversity in hiring ensure that they attract talent from a wide range of backgrounds. This can be achieved through unbiased hiring processes, diverse interview panels, and outreach efforts that connect with underrepresented groups. Once employees are hired, providing equal opportunities for career advancement is just as important. Clear promotion pathways, mentorship programs, and leadership development initiatives help create an environment where all employees have the opportunity to grow and succeed.

Employee engagement is another key factor in fostering inclusivity. Encouraging open communication, employee resource groups, and team collaboration strengthens workplace relationships and ensures that everyone's voice is heard. An inclusive culture is one where employees feel comfortable sharing their ideas, concerns, and experiences without fear of discrimination or exclusion. Regular feedback mechanisms, such as surveys and open forums, help organizations understand employee needs and make necessary improvements.

Workplace policies and benefits should also reflect a commitment to inclusivity. Flexible work arrangements, parental leave policies, and accommodations for individuals with disabilities create an environment where employees feel supported. Companies that actively promote work-life balance and mental well-being contribute to a healthier and more inclusive workforce.

A strong culture of inclusivity does not happen overnight; it requires continuous effort, education, and commitment. Businesses that embed inclusivity into their values and operations not only create a welcoming environment for employees but also gain a competitive advantage in attracting and retaining top talent. By prioritizing inclusivity, organizations build stronger teams, drive innovation, and achieve long-term success.

Leadership Development and Succession Planning

Leadership development and succession planning are vital for ensuring a business has a steady flow of skilled leaders ready to take over key roles and drive future growth. By focusing on nurturing potential leaders and planning for inevitable leadership transitions, companies can protect their operations against unexpected changes and adapt more effectively to new challenges.

Leadership development is about expanding individuals' capacity to fulfill leadership roles within organizations. This process includes identifying and nurturing potential leaders by equipping them with the necessary skills and experiences. Companies often implement a mix of training programs, mentorship, and stretch assignments to develop these crucial leadership qualities.

Training programs are essential for teaching theoretical knowledge and practical skills that future leaders need. Topics often include strategic decision-making, conflict resolution, and team management. Mentorship pairs less experienced employees with seasoned executives to provide invaluable insights and guidance, helping to transfer knowledge that isn't easily shared through formal training.

Stretch assignments challenge employees by placing them in demanding situations that require them to use and develop critical leadership skills like problem-solving, resilience, and project management. These experiences are vital for preparing employees to handle the complexities of leadership roles.

Succession planning, on the other hand, focuses on preparing suitable employees to replace key leaders as they depart or retire. This process begins with identifying potential leaders from within the current workforce, considering not only their existing skills and experiences but also their potential for leadership.

Once potential leaders are pinpointed, personalized development plans are created to ready them for their future roles. These plans typically blend targeted training, mentorship, and rotations across different company departments to provide a comprehensive leadership preparation experience.

Regular evaluations and feedback ensure these candidates are on the right track, allowing any gaps in skills or experience to be addressed before they step into their new roles. This ongoing assessment is crucial for smoothing the transition into leadership positions.

The strategic importance of these processes lies in their ability to ensure continuous leadership availability and contribute to a company's competitive edge. They help retain top talent by showing employees clear paths to leadership, enhancing job satisfaction, and improving retention rates. By preparing multiple employees for crucial roles, the company can maintain smooth operations even when unexpected changes in leadership occur, thus enhancing organizational resilience.

These strategies also drive innovation by bringing new ideas and perspectives to leadership roles, which can lead to significant advancements in company strategies and operations. The preparation and ongoing support provided to potential leaders enable them to bring fresh insights and drive necessary changes that keep the business ahead in a competitive market.

Leadership development and succession planning are not just about filling positions but are strategic processes critical for long-term success. They ensure that a company has a reliable pipeline of capable leaders who can not only sustain current success but also drive future growth. This approach to human capital management is crucial for any business looking to thrive in today's dynamic business environment.

Employee Engagement and Productivity

Employee engagement and productivity are tightly linked aspects of a successful business environment. Engaged employees are more likely to be productive, contributing positively to the organization's goals and outcomes. Understanding and fostering employee engagement can significantly enhance productivity and overall business performance.

Employee engagement refers to the level of enthusiasm and dedication an individual exhibits towards their job and company. Engaged employees are not just working for a paycheck or the next promotion but are part of a larger commitment to their team's and company's goals.

Engagement is influenced by several factors, including job satisfaction, organizational support, recognition, and opportunities for professional growth. When employees feel valued and supported, they are more likely to put in the effort that drives better business outcomes.

Productivity measures how efficiently tasks and goals are accomplished. Highly engaged employees tend to perform better because they are motivated to excel in their roles. They often go the extra mile to meet targets and contribute to the organization's objectives, which can lead to higher quality work and innovation.

Moreover, engaged employees typically have better attendance records and are less likely to leave the organization, reducing turnover costs and the disruption that can come with replacing experienced workers. They also foster a positive work environment that can further enhance the productivity of those around them.

Regular and transparent communication helps to build trust and align employees with the organization's vision. This includes not only disseminating information effectively across all levels but also ensuring that employee feedback is heard and valued.

Recognizing and rewarding employees for their hard work and achievements boosts morale and encourages high performance. Whether through formal reward systems or informal recognition practices, acknowledging employees' efforts plays a critical role in sustaining engagement.

Providing opportunities for professional growth and development can help maintain engagement levels. This includes training, mentorship programs, and clear pathways for career advancement within the organization.

Encouraging a balance between work and personal life helps prevent burnout and keeps employees motivated. Flexible working conditions, such as remote work options and flexible hours, can contribute to a more engaged and productive workforce.

Supporting employee health and wellness can improve engagement by showing that the organization cares about its employees' well-being. Programs can include mental health resources, fitness memberships, and wellness workshops.

The relationship between employee engagement and productivity is undeniable. Businesses that invest in creating an engaging work environment are likely to see improvements in productivity, employee retention, and overall profitability. By understanding the drivers of engagement and implementing strategies to foster an engaging work environment, organizations can reap substantial benefits that go beyond the bottom line.

Ethical Labor Practices and Compliance

Ethical labor practices and compliance are fundamental to maintaining a reputable and sustainable business. These principles ensure that a company treats its employees fairly, respects their rights, and adheres to all relevant laws and regulations. Embracing ethical labor practices not only aligns with legal obligations but also enhances company culture, boosts employee morale, and strengthens stakeholder relationships.

Ethical labor practices encompass a range of policies and actions designed to protect workers' rights and promote fair treatment within the workplace. This includes providing fair wages, ensuring safe working conditions, respecting working hours, and upholding anti-discrimination laws. Compliance refers to the company's adherence to local, national, and international laws that govern these aspects of employment.

A key component of ethical labor practices is the commitment to fair wages. This means compensating employees fairly based on their role, experience, and the industry standard. Fair wages are crucial not only for meeting legal standards but also for ensuring that employees feel valued for their contributions, which can directly influence their productivity and loyalty to the company.

Safe working conditions are another critical aspect. Businesses are required to provide a safe environment free of hazards. This includes proper training, safety equipment, and regular audits to ensure that safety standards are continuously met. Creating a safe workplace reduces the risk of injuries and illnesses, which can lead to better job satisfaction and reduced downtime due to absences.

Upholding anti-discrimination laws is vital for fostering an inclusive workplace. This involves implementing policies that prevent discrimination based on age, gender, race, religion, sexual orientation, or any other status. Companies must ensure that all employment practices, from hiring to promotions and terminations, are conducted fairly and without bias.

Compliance with labor laws is not just about avoiding legal repercussions; it's about building a foundation of trust and integrity. Companies that consistently demonstrate their commitment to legal and ethical standards are more likely to attract and retain top talent and receive support from consumers and other stakeholders.

Training and continuous education about ethical practices and legal requirements are crucial for maintaining compliance. Employees at all levels should be aware of the laws and ethical standards that affect their roles and be equipped to apply them in their daily activities.

Monitoring and enforcement mechanisms are essential to ensure ongoing compliance. This might involve regular audits, both internal and external, feedback mechanisms for employees to report unethical behavior or non-compliance, and clear consequences for violations.

Engaging with external stakeholders, such as local communities and industry groups, can also enhance a company's labor practices. This engagement can provide valuable insights into the societal expectations and additional standards that companies might strive to meet beyond basic compliance.

Ethical labor practices and compliance are not just regulatory requirements but are integral to building a sustainable and positive corporate culture. They enhance employee satisfaction, which in turn drives productivity and innovation. By investing in fair and safe working conditions and ensuring all legal obligations are met, businesses can build a strong reputation and sustainable success.

CHAPTER 22

Corporate Social Responsibility (CSR) & Sustainable Finance

Corporate Social Responsibility (CSR) and sustainable finance are increasingly becoming pivotal aspects of contemporary business strategies. These concepts reflect a growing recognition of the role businesses play in addressing social, environmental, and economic challenges. Through CSR, companies commit to operating in an ethical and sustainable manner that considers the interests of all stakeholders, including employees, communities, consumers, and the environment. Sustainable finance complements these efforts by prioritizing investments that yield long-term environmental, social, and economic benefits, thus driving progress towards sustainable global economies. This chapter explores how integrating CSR and sustainable finance into business operations can not only drive innovation and profitability but also contribute to a more equitable and sustainable world.

Foundations of CSR in Modern Business

Corporate Social Responsibility (CSR) has become a cornerstone in the modern business landscape. It signifies a company's dedication to behaving ethically and contributing to economic development while improving the quality of life for its workforce, their families, the local community, and society at large. At its core, CSR goes beyond compliance with regulatory requirements; it's about companies taking steps to conduct their business in a way that is ethical and sustainable.

Today's businesses are increasingly held accountable for their social, environmental, and economic impact. This shift is driven by consumers who demand transparency and responsibility from the brands they support. By focusing on CSR, companies can not only enhance their reputations but also strengthen their brands, build trust with consumers and other stakeholders, and attract and retain top talent. Moreover, a robust CSR strategy can lead to direct economic benefits, such as operational cost savings from efficiencies in resource use, and indirect benefits like improved employee morale and innovation.

A strong foundation in CSR for any business begins with understanding its key components: environmental responsibility, social equity, and economic viability. Businesses must assess their impact in these areas and set clear, achievable goals. Whether it's reducing carbon footprints, enhancing labor policies, engaging in fair trade, or contributing to community development, every action counts. Effective CSR requires a commitment to genuine acts of care, not just external displays of concern, and integrating these practices into every facet of operations, from supply chain management to employee relations and beyond.

In practice, implementing CSR can involve various initiatives, such as developing sustainable products, using resources more efficiently, providing safe and inclusive workplaces, and participating in community outreach programs. These activities are not only ethically rewarding but also position businesses to thrive in a rapidly changing global market increasingly influenced by social and environmental factors.

Environmental, Social, and Governance (ESG) Frameworks

Environmental, Social, and Governance (ESG) frameworks are becoming integral to modern business operations, guiding companies in their efforts to operate responsibly and sustainably. These frameworks help businesses measure, manage, and report on their impact on the environment, society, and their own governance practices. As businesses face increasing pressure from stakeholders, including investors, customers, and regulators, to demonstrate their commitment to sustainability, ESG frameworks provide a structured approach to addressing these demands.

Environmental considerations involve a company's impact on natural resources and ecosystems. This includes efforts to reduce carbon emissions, manage waste, conserve water, and protect biodiversity. Companies are increasingly recognizing the importance of environmental stewardship, not only as a duty to the planet but also as a factor that can significantly influence their financial performance and market reputation. For instance, companies in the manufacturing sector are investing in cleaner technologies and more efficient processes to minimize their environmental footprint, which can also reduce costs and improve profitability.

Social considerations focus on the company's relationships with employees, suppliers, customers, and the communities where it operates. This includes ensuring fair labor practices, protecting human rights, and contributing positively to local communities. For example, a company might implement programs to support employee well-being and development, engage in fair trade practices, or contribute to local economic development through education and training programs. Social responsibility is particularly scrutinized by consumers and can heavily influence brand loyalty and employee retention.

Governance considerations pertain to the systems, practices, and procedures that govern company operations and interactions with various stakeholders. Effective governance involves leadership, audits, board diversity, executive pay, and shareholder rights, among others. Strong governance ensures that a company operates transparently, ethically, and in accordance with regulatory and legal standards, which helps in building trust with investors and the public.

ESG frameworks vary widely but typically involve a combination of internal assessments and reporting based on external standards. Many companies adopt recognized frameworks such as the Global Reporting Initiative (GRI), the Sustainability Accounting Standards Board (SASB), or the Task Force on Climate-related Financial Disclosures (TCFD). These standards provide guidelines and tools for reporting on ESG performance, enabling companies to benchmark their progress and communicate it effectively to stakeholders.

Integrating ESG criteria into business operations requires substantial effort and commitment. Companies must first conduct thorough assessments of their current practices and impacts across ESG dimensions. This involves collecting data, engaging with stakeholders, and setting clear, measurable goals. For instance, a company might set specific targets for reducing greenhouse gas emissions, improving employee diversity, or enhancing board oversight.

Once goals are set, companies need to integrate ESG considerations into their strategic planning and decision-making processes. This might involve changing procurement practices to favor more sustainable suppliers, investing in employee training programs to improve social outcomes, or enhancing data security and governance practices. Companies also need to continuously monitor their performance against ESG criteria and adjust their strategies as necessary. This ongoing process not only helps companies address their immediate impacts but also prepares them to adapt to future regulatory changes and market expectations.

Moreover, transparent communication of ESG efforts and outcomes is crucial. Companies must not only track and measure their performance but also report it clearly and transparently to stakeholders. Effective reporting can enhance a company's credibility and can lead to greater stakeholder trust and engagement. It also positions companies favorably in the eyes of ESG-focused investors who are increasingly looking to allocate capital to businesses that demonstrate commitment to long-term sustainability.

ESG frameworks are not static, and they evolve as new challenges and opportunities emerge. Therefore, companies need to stay informed about global trends and best practices in ESG to continuously improve their strategies. Engaging with external experts, participating in industry forums, and leveraging advanced technologies can help companies stay at the forefront of ESG practices, ensuring their operations are both responsible and resilient in the face of global sustainability challenges.

Sustainable Investing and Impact Finance

Sustainable investing and impact finance are changing the way businesses and investors think about financial growth. Instead of focusing solely on profit, these approaches aim to generate positive social and environmental outcomes alongside financial returns. Investors are increasingly aware that long-term success depends not just on financial performance but also on how businesses contribute to society and the planet. As global challenges such as climate change, inequality, and resource scarcity continue to grow, sustainable investing and impact finance are becoming more important than ever.

Sustainable investing involves directing capital toward companies and projects that prioritize environmental, social, and governance (ESG) factors. Investors look beyond traditional financial indicators to evaluate how businesses manage their relationships with the environment, their employees, and their governance structures. Companies that actively work to reduce their carbon footprint, uphold ethical labor practices, and maintain transparent leadership are often seen as more resilient and forward-thinking. Sustainable investing does not mean sacrificing returns; in fact, many studies have shown that companies with strong ESG practices tend to perform well financially over the long term. This is because they are better prepared for regulatory changes, shifting consumer preferences, and potential risks related to environmental or social issues.

Impact finance takes this idea even further by targeting investments that create measurable and intentional positive change. Unlike traditional investments, where financial gain is the primary goal, impact finance focuses equally on social and environmental improvements. This type of financing supports projects in areas such as clean energy, affordable housing, healthcare, and education. Investors in impact finance seek not only financial returns but also tangible benefits for communities and ecosystems. Governments, foundations, and private investors all play a role in impact finance, supporting businesses and initiatives that address pressing global issues.

One key component of sustainable investing and impact finance is the use of green bonds and social bonds. Green bonds raise funds for projects that have clear environmental benefits, such as renewable energy infrastructure, sustainable agriculture, and water conservation. These bonds provide investors with an opportunity to support environmental initiatives while earning a return on their investment. Social bonds, on the other hand, fund projects aimed at improving social outcomes, such as affordable housing, access to education, and healthcare programs. Both types of bonds align investment capital with sustainability goals, making them an attractive option for investors looking to make a difference.

Another important strategy within sustainable investing is shareholder advocacy and engagement. Investors are using their influence to push companies toward responsible business practices. This can involve voting on shareholder resolutions related to climate policies, fair wages, or corporate transparency. When large institutional investors advocate for sustainable business strategies, companies are more likely to adopt policies that align with long-term social and environmental goals. Shareholder engagement ensures that businesses remain accountable and responsive to global sustainability challenges.

Technology has played a major role in advancing sustainable investing and impact finance. Digital platforms, artificial intelligence, and big data analytics help investors evaluate ESG factors more effectively. With better access to sustainability metrics, investors can make informed decisions about where to allocate their capital. Additionally, blockchain technology is being explored as a tool for increasing transparency in impact finance. By recording transactions on an immutable digital ledger, blockchain ensures that funds are used for their intended purposes, reducing the risk of fraud and mismanagement.

The rise of sustainable investing has also influenced how financial institutions operate. Many banks and asset managers now offer ESG-focused investment products, including mutual funds and exchange-traded funds (ETFs) that track socially responsible companies. These investment options make it easier for individuals and institutions to align their financial goals with their values. The demand for ESG-focused funds has surged in recent years, reflecting a broader shift in investor priorities.

Despite the growing popularity of sustainable investing and impact finance, challenges remain. One major issue is the lack of standardized ESG reporting. Different companies and industries use varying metrics to measure sustainability performance, making it difficult for investors to compare and evaluate opportunities. Efforts are being made to establish clearer guidelines and frameworks, such as those developed by the Global Reporting Initiative (GRI) and the Sustainability Accounting Standards Board (SASB). As these standards become more widely adopted, investors will have better tools to assess ESG performance.

Another challenge is the risk of "greenwashing," where companies present themselves as more sustainable than they actually are. Some businesses exaggerate or misrepresent their ESG efforts to attract socially conscious investors. To combat this, investors must conduct thorough research and rely on independent ESG ratings and audits. Transparency and accountability are crucial for ensuring that sustainable investments truly contribute to positive change.

The future of sustainable investing and impact finance looks promising. As awareness of global challenges increases, more investors are seeking opportunities that align with their values. Governments and regulatory bodies are also encouraging responsible investing by introducing policies that support sustainability initiatives. As a result, businesses that prioritize ESG factors are likely to gain a competitive advantage in the market.

For sustainable investing and impact finance to reach their full potential, collaboration between businesses, investors, policymakers, and consumers is essential. By working together, these groups can create financial systems that promote long-term prosperity while addressing environmental and social challenges. In doing so, they can ensure that economic growth is both responsible and inclusive, benefiting not just shareholders but society as a whole.

Circular Economy and Waste Reduction Strategies

A circular economy is an approach to production and consumption that focuses on reducing waste, reusing materials, and creating sustainable business practices. Unlike the traditional linear economy, where products are made, used, and then discarded, a circular economy aims to keep resources in use for as long as possible. This model benefits businesses, consumers, and the environment by minimizing waste, lowering costs, and reducing the strain on natural resources. As industries and governments recognize the need for more sustainable economic practices, circular economy strategies are becoming more common in businesses of all sizes.

Waste reduction is a key part of the circular economy. Companies are shifting away from disposable products and designing goods that can be repaired, refurbished, or recycled. Many businesses are adopting closed-loop systems, where materials from old products are collected and used to create new ones. This reduces the demand for raw materials and cuts down on the environmental impact of manufacturing. Large corporations and small businesses alike are investing in better waste management processes, including using biodegradable packaging, optimizing supply chains, and developing take-back programs where consumers can return used products for recycling.

One of the most effective ways businesses can reduce waste is through product design. By creating durable, repairable, and modular products, companies can extend the lifespan of their goods. Many electronics manufacturers, for example, are developing devices with easily replaceable parts so that customers can repair them instead of discarding them. In the fashion industry, brands are using sustainable fabrics and promoting second-hand clothing markets to reduce textile waste. Designing with sustainability in mind helps businesses build long-term relationships with consumers who value environmental responsibility.

Another important aspect of a circular economy is the sharing economy. This model encourages the use of shared resources instead of individual ownership. Car-sharing services, tool rental businesses, and coworking spaces are all examples of how companies are making better use of resources by allowing multiple people to access the same product or service. By reducing the need for constant production of new goods, the sharing economy helps lower waste and conserve raw materials. Businesses that adopt this model can create new revenue streams while also reducing their environmental impact.

Recycling and upcycling play a major role in waste reduction. Many companies are working to improve their recycling processes by ensuring that materials can be easily separated and reused. Some businesses are even turning waste into new products, a practice known as upcycling. For example, food companies are using leftover fruit and vegetable scraps to create natural dyes or compostable packaging. Similarly, plastic waste is being transformed into everything from clothing to construction materials. By finding innovative ways to repurpose waste, businesses can create value while reducing their environmental footprint.

Technology is also helping businesses move toward a circular economy. Digital platforms allow companies to track and optimize resource use, reducing waste at every stage of production. Blockchain technology is being explored as a way to improve transparency in supply chains, ensuring that materials are sourced sustainably and disposed of responsibly. Artificial intelligence and machine learning are helping companies identify inefficiencies in their operations, allowing them to cut down on waste and make better use of resources. As technology continues to evolve, it will provide even more opportunities for businesses to adopt circular economy principles.

Collaboration between businesses, governments, and consumers is essential for the success of a circular economy. Governments are introducing policies that encourage waste reduction, such as banning single-use plastics, setting recycling targets, and offering incentives for sustainable business practices. Consumers are also playing a role by supporting brands that prioritize sustainability and making more conscious purchasing decisions. Businesses that work with policymakers and customers to implement circular economy strategies will be better positioned for long-term success.

Financial benefits also make a strong case for businesses to invest in waste reduction and circular economy practices. Reducing waste can lower production costs, improve efficiency, and attract environmentally conscious consumers. Investors are increasingly looking for companies that integrate sustainability into their business models, recognizing that these companies are more likely to thrive in the long run. By prioritizing resource efficiency and waste reduction, businesses can not only contribute to a healthier planet but also strengthen their market position.

Shifting to a circular economy requires a change in mindset. Instead of viewing waste as a problem, businesses should see it as an opportunity for innovation and value creation. By rethinking how products are designed, manufactured, and used, companies can develop more sustainable business models that benefit both their bottom line and the environment. Waste reduction strategies are no longer just an ethical choice—they are becoming a necessity in a world where resources are limited, and environmental concerns are growing. Businesses that take action now will not only reduce their environmental impact but also build a more resilient and competitive future.

CHAPTER 23

Global Business Strategies & Cross-Cultural Dynamics

Operating in the global marketplace presents both opportunities and challenges for businesses looking to expand beyond their home countries. Companies that successfully enter international markets must navigate cultural differences, regulatory requirements, economic conditions, and competitive landscapes that vary widely from one region to another. Understanding global business strategies is essential for businesses aiming to establish a strong presence in foreign markets while managing risks effectively. Cross-cultural dynamics also play a crucial role in international business, as communication styles, negotiation tactics, and consumer preferences differ across cultures. Companies that adapt their strategies to align with local customs, business practices, and market demands can build stronger relationships, enhance their brand reputation, and achieve long-term success on a global scale. As technology continues to bridge geographic barriers, businesses must develop strategies that balance global efficiency with local responsiveness, ensuring that they remain competitive in an increasingly interconnected world.

Navigating International Market Entry

Expanding into international markets is a significant step for any business, requiring careful planning, strategic decision-making, and a clear understanding of the target market. Entering a foreign market is not as simple as replicating an existing business model in a new location. It involves studying economic conditions, consumer behavior, legal and regulatory requirements, and competition. Every country has unique market dynamics, and companies that wish to succeed must take the time to understand the challenges and opportunities that come with operating in a new environment.

Before making any move into an international market, businesses must conduct thorough market research. Understanding the demand for products or services is essential, along with identifying the preferences and purchasing behaviors of potential customers. The level of competition in the new market is another key factor. Some industries are highly competitive, with well-established local players, while others may have gaps that a foreign company can fill. A deep analysis of customer needs, existing competitors, and industry trends helps businesses determine whether entering the market is a viable opportunity.

Choosing the right market entry strategy is another crucial step. There are several ways a business can establish itself in a foreign market, and each method has its advantages and risks. Exporting is one of the simplest and most cost-effective ways to enter an international market. Businesses can sell their products overseas without setting up physical operations in the target country. However, exporting comes with challenges such as tariffs, shipping costs, and the need to find reliable local distributors. Another approach is licensing or franchising, where a business grants the rights to a local company to use its brand, products, or business model. This can reduce risks and allow for faster expansion, but it requires finding trustworthy partners who will maintain the quality and reputation of the brand.

For companies that want greater control over their operations, setting up a joint venture or forming strategic partnerships with local businesses can be a beneficial option. Joint ventures allow businesses to share resources, knowledge, and market access with local firms, helping to overcome regulatory barriers and cultural differences. However, partnerships require careful negotiation to ensure that both parties benefit and that conflicts are minimized. Establishing a wholly-owned subsidiary is another market entry strategy, where a company sets up its own operations in a foreign market. While this provides full control over the business, it also involves higher costs and risks. It requires significant investment in infrastructure, local hiring, and compliance with local regulations.

Understanding the legal and regulatory environment is another key aspect of international expansion. Different countries have different laws regarding taxation, labor regulations, intellectual property protection, and business registration. Companies must ensure they comply with local laws to avoid legal complications. Some governments impose restrictions on foreign businesses, requiring them to operate through local partnerships or comply with industry-specific regulations. Engaging legal experts who specialize in international business can help businesses navigate these complexities.

Cultural differences also play a significant role in international market entry. What works in one country may not necessarily work in another. From marketing strategies to customer service approaches, businesses must be aware of cultural expectations and adapt accordingly. Language barriers, traditions, consumer preferences, and negotiation styles all influence how a company is perceived in a foreign market. A marketing campaign that resonates with one culture may be ineffective or even offensive in another. To succeed, businesses need to localize their strategies, ensuring that their branding, messaging, and overall approach align with the cultural values of the target market.

Pricing strategies also require careful planning. A product that is considered affordable in one country may be seen as too expensive in another. Pricing should be based on factors such as local income levels, competitor pricing, cost of goods sold, and perceived value. Businesses must also consider foreign exchange fluctuations, import duties, and taxes, which can affect profitability.

Logistics and supply chain management are other important considerations when entering an international market. Reliable distribution channels, warehousing facilities, and transportation networks are essential for delivering products efficiently. Some markets have underdeveloped infrastructure, which can create delays and additional costs. Businesses must assess how they will manage inventory, maintain product quality, and ensure smooth delivery to customers.

Building brand awareness in a new market is another challenge. Unlike in their home country, businesses entering a foreign market often start with little to no brand recognition. Effective marketing strategies, local partnerships, and targeted advertising campaigns can help build credibility and trust. Social media, influencer collaborations, and digital marketing can be valuable tools for reaching international audiences. Establishing relationships with local media and community organizations can also enhance brand visibility.

Customer service and support are also key factors in international market entry. Businesses must ensure that they provide excellent customer experiences that meet the expectations of local consumers. This includes offering multilingual customer support, clear return policies, and efficient complaint resolution. Providing localized services helps build a positive reputation and fosters long-term customer loyalty.

Despite the challenges, entering an international market can lead to significant growth and profitability if done correctly. Companies that take the time to plan their expansion carefully, conduct thorough research, and adapt their strategies to meet local market conditions increase their chances of long-term success. Expanding into new regions provides access to larger customer bases, greater revenue potential, and opportunities for innovation. However, businesses must remain flexible, continuously monitor market conditions, and be willing to adjust their strategies based on real-world experiences. International expansion is not just about selling products or services in another country; it is about building sustainable and meaningful relationships with customers, employees, and partners in a new and diverse business environment.

Cultural Intelligence in Business Negotiations

Successful business negotiations require more than just strong arguments and persuasive communication. When dealing with international partners, understanding cultural differences plays a key role in reaching agreements and building long-term relationships. Cultural intelligence is the ability to recognize and adapt to different cultural perspectives, behaviors, and values. In a global business environment, where negotiations involve people from diverse backgrounds, cultural intelligence helps businesses navigate complexities, avoid misunderstandings, and foster mutual respect.

One of the biggest challenges in international negotiations is communication style. Different cultures have distinct ways of expressing agreement, disagreement, and intent. In some cultures, such as those in the United States and Germany, direct communication is valued. Businesspeople are expected to speak clearly, state their positions openly, and be straightforward in addressing concerns. In contrast, in many Asian cultures, indirect communication is preferred. Instead of saying "no" outright, negotiators might use subtle language or avoid direct rejection to maintain harmony. Without cultural awareness, a negotiator from a direct-speaking culture may misinterpret indirect responses as agreement when, in reality, the other party is hesitant or unwilling to proceed.

Another important cultural difference is the approach to building relationships. In some cultures, particularly in Western countries, business negotiations focus primarily on contracts, financial terms, and legal details. Once a deal is finalized, the relationship between the parties may not extend beyond the business transaction. However, in many other parts of the world, especially in Latin America, the Middle East, and parts of Asia, building trust and personal relationships is essential before discussing business details. Negotiations often begin with casual conversations, shared meals, and discussions about personal matters. Rushing into business without establishing trust may be seen as disrespectful or unprofessional.

Negotiation styles also vary based on cultural attitudes toward hierarchy and decision-making. In some cultures, such as in Japan or Saudi Arabia, businesses operate with strict hierarchies, and decisions are made by top executives after careful deliberation. Junior team members may not have the authority to negotiate or make commitments on behalf of their company. In contrast, in cultures with a more egalitarian approach, such as those in Scandinavia or Australia, decision-making is often shared among team members. Understanding these differences is crucial because a negotiator who expects immediate decisions may become frustrated when dealing with a hierarchy-driven culture, where decisions take time and require multiple levels of approval.

Time perception also plays a significant role in international negotiations. In some cultures, time is viewed rigidly, and punctuality is highly valued. Meetings start and end on time, and sticking to the agenda is expected. This is common in countries such as Germany, Switzerland, and the United States. However, in other cultures, such as those in the Middle East, Africa, and parts of Latin America, flexibility in scheduling is more common. Business meetings may start late, last longer than planned, or be rescheduled at the last minute. A negotiator from a time-conscious culture may interpret these differences as inefficiency or a lack of professionalism, while for the other party, such flexibility is a normal part of business interactions.

The way conflict and disagreement are handled also varies across cultures. In some cultures, open debate and argumentation are seen as part of a productive discussion. Disagreements are expressed openly, and it is normal to challenge ideas and negotiate aggressively. In contrast, in more collectivist cultures, avoiding conflict and maintaining group harmony is a priority. Disagreements may be expressed subtly or indirectly, and negotiators may use diplomatic language to soften criticism. Failing to recognize these differences can lead to frustration or even the breakdown of negotiations.

Nonverbal communication is another critical aspect of cultural intelligence in business negotiations. Body language, eye contact, hand gestures, and personal space expectations vary widely across cultures. In the United States, maintaining eye contact is often a sign of confidence and honesty, while in some Asian cultures, prolonged eye contact may be considered aggressive or disrespectful. Similarly, handshakes, bowing, or even the appropriate use of silence carry different meanings in different parts of the world. Misinterpreting these nonverbal cues can lead to unintended misunderstandings or offense.

Cultural intelligence is not about memorizing rules for each culture but about developing an open-minded and adaptable mindset. Business negotiators who take the time to learn about their counterparts' cultural backgrounds, customs, and business etiquette can build stronger relationships and improve the likelihood of successful deals. Companies that invest in cultural training for their employees gain a competitive advantage in international business, as they can navigate negotiations more effectively and avoid costly mistakes.

Incorporating cultural intelligence into business negotiations requires preparation and flexibility. Before entering negotiations, it is essential to research the cultural norms of the other party, seek advice from cultural experts or local business partners, and remain observant during interactions. Demonstrating respect for cultural differences and being willing to adapt negotiation styles shows professionalism and commitment to long-term collaboration. By prioritizing cultural awareness, businesses can strengthen international partnerships, build mutual trust, and achieve successful outcomes in a globally connected marketplace.

Managing Geopolitical Risks and Trade Barriers

International business operates in a world that is constantly changing due to political shifts, regulatory changes, and economic policies. Geopolitical risks and trade barriers are some of the most significant challenges businesses face when expanding or operating across borders. Political instability, trade restrictions, tariffs, sanctions, and economic conflicts between nations can create uncertainty for businesses, making it difficult to plan for long-term success.

Companies that understand these risks and develop strategies to manage them can protect their investments, reduce losses, and continue operations even in unpredictable environments.

One of the most pressing geopolitical risks is political instability in different regions. Governments can change leadership, introduce new economic policies, or experience social unrest, all of which can disrupt business operations. Political instability may lead to sudden changes in trade policies, nationalization of industries, or shifts in diplomatic relations that impact cross-border transactions. Businesses that rely on supply chains in politically unstable countries must be prepared for possible disruptions, including delays in shipments, unexpected regulatory changes, or even the seizure of assets by the government. Companies can manage these risks by diversifying their supply chains, investing in multiple markets rather than relying on a single country, and forming partnerships with local businesses that understand the political landscape.

Trade barriers, including tariffs and import/export restrictions, can significantly affect international businesses. Governments impose tariffs on imported goods to protect domestic industries or as a response to economic disputes with other nations. These additional costs can make foreign goods less competitive, leading to reduced demand. For example, when the United States and China imposed tariffs on each other's goods during the trade war, businesses in both countries faced higher costs and supply chain disruptions. Companies affected by tariffs often need to adjust their pricing strategies, source materials from alternative suppliers, or shift production to countries with more favorable trade agreements.

Sanctions are another form of trade barrier that businesses must carefully navigate. Governments impose sanctions to restrict trade with certain countries, organizations, or individuals due to political conflicts, human rights violations, or security concerns. Companies that violate sanctions, even unintentionally, can face severe legal and financial consequences. For example, global banks and corporations have been fined billions of dollars for doing business with sanctioned entities. To avoid such penalties, businesses must stay informed about international sanctions, conduct thorough due diligence on business partners, and implement strict compliance measures to ensure they are not engaging in prohibited transactions.

Protectionist policies can also create challenges for businesses operating internationally. Some governments adopt policies that prioritize domestic industries by restricting foreign investment, imposing local hiring requirements, or enforcing strict regulatory standards. While these policies may be intended to boost the local economy, they can make it more difficult for foreign businesses to compete. Companies looking to enter markets with protectionist policies must carefully analyze the regulatory landscape, establish local partnerships, and ensure compliance with government requirements to maintain their operations.

Geopolitical risks are not limited to direct government actions; regional conflicts and diplomatic tensions also impact businesses. Tensions between neighboring countries can disrupt trade routes, increase security concerns, and create uncertainty in the marketplace. Businesses involved in international logistics and transportation must be prepared for potential disruptions caused by conflicts or border disputes. In some cases, geopolitical instability can also lead to currency fluctuations, making financial transactions riskier. Companies must monitor global developments closely and adopt flexible strategies, such as using hedging mechanisms to protect against currency volatility.

Businesses that operate internationally must develop comprehensive risk management strategies to address geopolitical challenges and trade barriers. One approach is to diversify operations across multiple regions to reduce dependence on any single market. If one country imposes trade restrictions or experiences political instability, businesses with operations in other countries can shift resources and continue operating without major disruptions. Companies should also establish strong relationships with local governments, industry associations, and trade organizations to stay informed about regulatory changes and potential risks.

Investing in legal and compliance expertise is essential for businesses navigating international trade regulations. Companies must ensure that their contracts, supply chain agreements, and financial transactions comply with international laws and trade policies. Many businesses hire legal teams or external consultants specializing in international trade law to help them manage compliance and mitigate risks.

Technology also plays a vital role in managing geopolitical risks and trade barriers. Digital supply chain tracking, real-time trade monitoring, and artificial intelligence-based risk analysis allow businesses to identify potential disruptions before they occur. Advanced analytics can help companies assess the likelihood of trade barriers being introduced and adjust their business strategies accordingly.

Strong risk management planning is critical for businesses looking to thrive in a complex global environment. Companies that stay informed about political developments, engage with local stakeholders, and adopt flexible strategies will be better positioned to overcome trade barriers and geopolitical challenges. While global business presents risks, companies that anticipate challenges and implement proactive measures can continue to grow, adapt, and succeed in an unpredictable world.

Localization vs. Globalization of Brands

Expanding a brand internationally presents businesses with a crucial decision: should they localize their brand to fit the specific culture, preferences, and consumer behavior of each market, or should they maintain a standardized, global identity? Both localization and globalization strategies offer unique advantages and challenges, and finding the right balance is key to long-term success in international markets. Companies that understand when to adapt their brand to local markets and when to maintain a consistent global identity can build strong connections with consumers while maintaining operational efficiency.

Localization focuses on tailoring a brand's products, messaging, and marketing strategies to align with the cultural norms, language, and consumer behavior of a specific region. This approach recognizes that different markets have distinct preferences and expectations, and it allows businesses to create a more personalized and relevant experience for consumers. Localization can include adapting product names, packaging, advertising messages, and even product features to better suit a specific market. For example, global fast-food chains often modify their menus to reflect local tastes. McDonald's offers McSpaghetti in the Philippines, paneer-based burgers in India, and shrimp burgers in Japan, catering to the culinary preferences of these regions. By doing so, the company ensures that its products resonate with local consumers while maintaining its core brand identity.

Cultural sensitivity plays a crucial role in localization. A marketing campaign that is effective in one country may not have the same impact in another due to differences in language, values, and traditions. Brands that fail to consider these cultural factors risk alienating potential customers or, worse, offending them. For example, Pepsi once faced backlash in China for a slogan that was mistranslated to mean "Pepsi brings your ancestors back from the dead," a major cultural misstep. Effective localization requires extensive market research, collaboration with local experts, and a deep understanding of the cultural landscape to ensure that branding efforts align with consumer expectations.

Globalization, on the other hand, involves maintaining a consistent brand image, message, and product offering across all markets. This strategy emphasizes brand uniformity, creating a recognizable identity that consumers can trust, regardless of location. Companies that pursue globalization benefit from economies of scale, as they can streamline production, marketing, and distribution processes without making significant modifications for each region. Apple is a prime example of a company that successfully follows a globalization strategy. The design, branding, and marketing of iPhones, MacBooks, and other Apple products remain largely the same worldwide, reinforcing the brand's premium image and technological innovation. Consumers associate Apple with high-quality, user-friendly products, and the consistency of its brand messaging strengthens customer loyalty on a global scale.

Globalization allows businesses to build strong brand equity by creating a uniform customer experience. Consumers who travel internationally often seek familiar brands, and a globally consistent brand helps build trust and recognition. Companies that maintain a strong global presence can also capitalize on the power of digital marketing, using the same advertising campaigns and promotional strategies across multiple countries. This approach reduces costs and ensures that a brand's message remains cohesive. However, globalization does come with risks. A standardized approach may not always resonate with local consumers who have specific preferences and expectations. Some markets may reject a product or service that feels too foreign or does not align with cultural norms. For instance, while Starbucks has successfully expanded globally, it initially struggled in Australia, where the coffee culture is dominated by independent cafés and a preference for high-quality, locally roasted coffee. The company's standardized approach failed to appeal to Australian consumers, leading to the closure of many Starbucks locations in the region.

Finding the right balance between localization and globalization is essential for brands looking to expand internationally. Some companies adopt a "glocalization" approach, which combines global consistency with local adaptations. This strategy allows businesses to maintain a strong global brand identity while making necessary adjustments to cater to specific markets. Coca-Cola is an example of a company that excels at glocalization. While its brand remains globally recognizable, the company adapts its flavors, packaging, and marketing messages to suit local tastes. In Japan, Coca-Cola introduced unique beverage flavors such as green tea and peach, appealing to local consumers while maintaining its iconic brand presence.

Technology plays a significant role in helping businesses navigate localization and globalization strategies. Data analytics and artificial intelligence allow companies to gather insights on consumer behavior, preferences, and market trends in different regions. By leveraging this data, businesses can make informed decisions on whether to adapt their products and marketing efforts or maintain a consistent global brand presence. Social media and digital platforms also provide opportunities for brands to engage with local audiences while maintaining a unified global message. Companies can use targeted advertising to tailor content for different markets while ensuring their core brand identity remains intact.

Ultimately, the decision between localization and globalization depends on a company's goals, industry, and target markets. Businesses that prioritize efficiency and brand consistency may lean towards globalization, while those seeking deeper connections with local consumers may invest in localization efforts. A flexible approach that combines elements of both strategies can often yield the best results, allowing businesses to maintain a strong global identity while adapting to the unique needs of local markets.

Ethical Dilemmas in Global Operations

Operating a business on a global scale presents companies with a range of ethical dilemmas that can be challenging to navigate. Different countries have distinct cultural norms, legal systems, labor practices, and environmental regulations, which can sometimes conflict with a company's values or ethical standards. Businesses that expand internationally must carefully consider the ethical implications of their decisions, balancing profitability with social responsibility. Failing to address ethical dilemmas properly can result in reputational damage, legal issues, and loss of consumer trust.

One of the most common ethical challenges in global operations is labor practices and working conditions. In some regions, labor laws are less stringent than in developed countries, allowing companies to hire workers at extremely low wages and under poor conditions. Some multinational corporations have been criticized for outsourcing production to factories where workers face long hours, unsafe environments, and unfair wages. Ethical businesses must ensure that their suppliers and subcontractors adhere to fair labor standards, even in countries where local laws may not require it. Companies that ignore these concerns risk consumer backlash, as seen in past controversies involving major brands accused of using sweatshops.

Bribery and corruption present another significant ethical dilemma. In certain regions, bribery is an unofficial but expected part of doing business, influencing government officials or business partners to secure contracts or bypass regulatory hurdles. While some countries have strict anti-corruption laws, such as the U.S. Foreign Corrupt Practices Act (FCPA) and the UK Bribery Act, enforcement varies globally. Businesses must decide whether to comply with ethical standards and risk losing opportunities in corrupt markets or participate in questionable practices to gain a competitive edge. Companies that engage in corruption not only face legal consequences but also damage their reputation, making it difficult to maintain long-term success.

Environmental responsibility is a growing ethical concern for global businesses. Some countries have weak environmental regulations, allowing companies to exploit natural resources without significant restrictions. This can lead to deforestation, water pollution, and other environmental damage. Ethical companies take proactive measures to minimize their environmental impact by adopting sustainable practices, reducing carbon emissions, and ensuring responsible waste management. While these measures may increase costs in the short term, they contribute to long-term sustainability and help maintain consumer trust.

Cultural sensitivity and marketing ethics are also crucial considerations. What is considered acceptable advertising or business behavior in one country may be offensive or inappropriate in another. Some companies have faced criticism for marketing campaigns that fail to respect local cultural or religious values. Ethical businesses invest in understanding the cultural norms of the markets they operate in, ensuring that their messaging aligns with local expectations. Additionally, global businesses must consider whether their products or services contribute positively to society. For instance, fast-food chains and sugary beverage companies have been scrutinized for promoting unhealthy lifestyles in countries struggling with rising obesity rates.

Tax avoidance and financial transparency pose ethical challenges for multinational corporations. Some global companies use legal loopholes to shift profits to low-tax jurisdictions, minimizing their tax liability. While these practices may be technically legal, they raise questions about corporate social responsibility. Governments and advocacy groups have increasingly called for companies to pay their fair share of taxes in the countries where they operate. Ethical businesses prioritize financial transparency and contribute to the economies they benefit from, rather than exploiting legal gaps to avoid taxation.

Respecting human rights is another critical ethical responsibility in global operations. Some industries, such as mining, agriculture, and manufacturing, have been linked to human rights abuses, including forced labor and child labor. Businesses must ensure that their supply chains are free from exploitative practices by conducting regular audits and partnering with ethical suppliers. Companies that fail to address human rights concerns risk legal action, consumer boycotts, and severe reputational damage.

Finding the right balance between profit and ethical responsibility requires strong corporate governance and a commitment to ethical leadership. Companies that prioritize ethical decision-making not only contribute to a better global business environment but also build long-term customer loyalty and brand trust. Consumers and investors are increasingly favoring companies that demonstrate social responsibility, making ethical business practices not just a moral choice but also a strategic advantage. Businesses that integrate ethics into their global operations can navigate complex challenges while maintaining credibility and long-term success in the international market.

Technology's Role in Bridging Cultural Gaps

Technology has transformed the way businesses operate across different cultures, making it easier to connect, communicate, and collaborate on a global scale. As companies expand internationally, they often encounter cultural differences that can impact negotiations, teamwork, and overall business relationships. Technology plays a crucial role in bridging these cultural gaps by facilitating communication, enhancing collaboration, and fostering a deeper understanding of diverse perspectives. Businesses that leverage technology effectively can overcome language barriers, streamline cross-border operations, and create inclusive work environments that respect cultural differences.

One of the most significant ways technology helps bridge cultural gaps is through communication tools. Language barriers have historically been a major challenge for international businesses, but advancements in translation software and real-time language processing have made it easier for people from different linguistic backgrounds to communicate effectively. AI-powered translation apps, speech recognition tools, and multilingual chatbots enable businesses to engage with international clients and partners in their native languages. Video conferencing platforms also offer live captioning and translation features, making virtual meetings more inclusive and ensuring that language differences do not hinder collaboration.

Digital collaboration platforms have revolutionized the way multinational teams work together. Cloud-based tools allow employees from different countries to share documents, track project progress, and coordinate tasks in real time. Platforms like Slack, Microsoft Teams, and Google Workspace provide seamless communication channels, reducing the challenges of time zone differences and geographic distance. These tools promote transparency and inclusivity, ensuring that every team member, regardless of location, has equal access to information and the opportunity to contribute to business goals.

Cultural awareness and sensitivity are essential in global business, and technology has made it easier to educate employees on cultural differences. Online training programs, virtual reality (VR) simulations, and artificial intelligence-driven cultural intelligence platforms help employees understand cultural norms, business etiquette, and social expectations in different regions. By using these tools, businesses can train their workforce to navigate cultural diversity with greater sensitivity and awareness. This not only improves cross-cultural interactions but also helps prevent misunderstandings that could damage business relationships.

E-commerce and digital marketing strategies have also benefited from technology's ability to bridge cultural gaps. Companies can now analyze consumer behavior in different markets using data analytics and AI-driven insights. This allows businesses to tailor their marketing messages, product offerings, and customer experiences to align with the preferences and expectations of diverse audiences. Social media platforms provide businesses with a direct way to engage with customers from various cultural backgrounds, fostering meaningful connections and enabling brands to localize their messaging effectively.

Artificial intelligence and machine learning play a crucial role in cultural adaptation by analyzing regional trends and customer preferences. AI-driven recommendation engines help businesses customize their offerings for specific markets, ensuring that cultural sensitivities are respected. For example, streaming services like Netflix use AI to recommend content based on viewing habits in different countries, while e-commerce platforms adjust product recommendations based on local shopping trends. This level of personalization enhances customer satisfaction and helps businesses build strong relationships with international audiences.

Technology also supports cross-cultural negotiations by providing data-driven insights and predictive analytics. Business leaders can use AI-powered negotiation tools to analyze market conditions, assess cultural differences, and develop strategies that align with local business practices. Virtual reality and augmented reality (AR) technologies allow companies to simulate real-world business interactions, helping executives prepare for negotiations in different cultural contexts. These advancements enable businesses to approach international deals with greater confidence and cultural awareness, improving the chances of successful outcomes.

The role of technology in fostering cultural inclusivity extends to employee engagement and workplace diversity. Remote work solutions have enabled businesses to build globally distributed teams, allowing employees from different cultural backgrounds to collaborate without the need for physical relocation. Virtual team-building activities, diversity and inclusion training programs, and AI-driven bias detection tools help companies create inclusive work environments that value and respect cultural differences. By leveraging these technologies, businesses can attract top talent from around the world and promote a workplace culture that embraces diversity.

Despite its many advantages, technology also presents challenges in bridging cultural gaps. Differences in digital infrastructure, internet accessibility, and technological literacy can create disparities in how businesses engage with different markets. Companies must ensure that their technology-driven strategies are inclusive and accessible to all cultural groups. Additionally, businesses must be mindful of cultural sensitivities when using AI and automation, as biases in algorithms can inadvertently reinforce stereotypes or misunderstand cultural nuances.

The integration of technology into global business operations has reshaped the way companies navigate cultural diversity. From communication tools and digital collaboration platforms to AI-driven cultural intelligence and data analytics, technology provides businesses with the resources they need to connect with international markets effectively. By embracing technological innovations, companies can overcome cultural barriers, foster stronger global relationships, and create an inclusive business environment that values diversity. As technology continues to evolve, its role in bridging cultural gaps will become even more critical in shaping the future of international business.

CHAPTER 24

Technology & Innovation in Finance

Technology has transformed the financial industry, reshaping the way businesses and consumers manage money, make transactions, and access financial services. Innovation in finance has led to the rise of digital banking, automation, artificial intelligence, and blockchain, making financial processes faster, more secure, and accessible to a global audience. Traditional banking models have evolved, with fintech companies introducing new solutions that improve efficiency, reduce costs, and enhance customer experiences. The growing reliance on digital payments, data-driven decision-making, and decentralized finance highlights how technology continues to redefine the financial landscape. Businesses, financial institutions, and regulators must adapt to these changes while ensuring security, compliance, and sustainability in the rapidly evolving financial ecosystem.

Fintech Disruption and Digital Banking

Financial technology, or fintech, has reshaped the banking industry, offering faster, more accessible, and user-friendly financial services. Traditional banking once required customers to visit physical branches for basic transactions, but fintech innovations have made it possible to manage accounts, transfer money, apply for loans, and invest — all from a smartphone. Digital banking has eliminated many of the inefficiencies of traditional finance, making banking services available 24/7 without the need for in-person visits.

One of the most significant changes brought by fintech is the introduction of mobile banking apps. These platforms allow customers to check balances, pay bills, send money, and even trade stocks with just a few taps. Digital wallets and payment apps have further transformed how people handle transactions, reducing dependence on cash and even physical cards. Services like Apple Pay, Google Pay, and PayPal make it easy to complete purchases both online and in stores. Peer-to-peer payment systems have also become widely used, enabling instant money transfers between individuals without the need for bank intermediaries.

Lending has also been revolutionized by fintech. Digital lending platforms use algorithms and artificial intelligence to assess creditworthiness, making loan approval processes much faster than traditional banks. Instead of waiting weeks for approval, borrowers can receive funds within hours or even minutes. Fintech companies also offer alternative lending models such as peer-to-peer lending, where individuals can lend money directly to borrowers without a traditional financial institution acting as a middleman.

Blockchain technology has played a key role in digital banking by enhancing security and transparency. Many fintech companies use blockchain to facilitate secure transactions, reduce fraud, and provide decentralized financial services. Cryptocurrencies have emerged as a result of blockchain, offering an alternative form of digital money that operates outside traditional banking systems. Some banks have begun exploring blockchain for secure cross-border payments, reducing transaction times and costs associated with international transfers.

Another major development in digital banking is the rise of neobanks, which are online-only banks without physical branches. These banks offer lower fees, higher interest rates on savings, and seamless digital experiences. Unlike traditional banks, neobanks operate entirely through mobile apps and web platforms, appealing to younger generations and tech-savvy consumers. While they provide many of the same services as conventional banks, they often partner with established financial institutions to ensure regulatory compliance and security.

Regulatory challenges remain a major factor in the expansion of fintech and digital banking. Governments and financial authorities continue to develop policies to ensure that these innovations are safe for consumers while preventing fraud and money laundering. As the industry grows, regulators must find a balance between fostering innovation and maintaining financial stability.

Artificial intelligence and machine learning are also playing a crucial role in shaping the future of digital banking. These technologies help banks detect fraud, improve customer service through chatbots, and personalize financial recommendations based on user behavior. AI-driven tools can analyze spending patterns, provide budgeting advice, and even suggest investment opportunities, making banking more interactive and customer-centric.

The evolution of fintech and digital banking has created financial inclusion opportunities for people who previously lacked access to banking services. In many developing regions, digital banking has allowed individuals to participate in the economy without needing a traditional bank account. Mobile banking services in countries with limited banking infrastructure have enabled millions to save, invest, and make payments securely.

While fintech has revolutionized banking, challenges remain. Cybersecurity threats, data breaches, and privacy concerns are ongoing risks in the digital finance world. As banking becomes more digital, the need for stronger security measures grows. Financial institutions must continuously invest in advanced encryption, biometric authentication, and fraud detection systems to protect customers from cyber threats.

The rapid growth of fintech is shaping a future where banking is more accessible, efficient, and tailored to individual needs. Digital banking continues to evolve, integrating emerging technologies to improve services and security. As the financial industry adapts, traditional banks must either embrace these innovations or risk becoming obsolete. The transformation of banking through fintech is not just a trend—it is the new standard, defining how financial services will operate in the years to come.

Artificial Intelligence in Financial Decision-Making

Artificial intelligence has become a powerful tool in financial decision-making, transforming how businesses, banks, and investors analyze data, manage risks, and make strategic choices. Traditional financial decision-making relied heavily on manual data analysis, historical trends, and expert judgment, which could be time-consuming and prone to human error. AI has introduced automation, predictive analytics, and real-time insights, making financial processes faster, more efficient, and more accurate.

One of the most significant ways AI is changing financial decision-making is through data analysis. AI-powered systems can process vast amounts of financial data in seconds, identifying patterns and trends that humans might miss. This capability is particularly useful in stock market predictions, where AI models analyze past market behavior, economic indicators, and news sentiment to forecast potential price movements. Hedge funds and investment firms use AI-driven algorithms to optimize trading strategies, reduce risks, and maximize returns.

AI is also improving risk assessment in finance. Banks and lenders use machine learning models to evaluate creditworthiness, determining whether an individual or business qualifies for a loan. Instead of relying solely on credit scores, AI considers alternative data sources such as spending habits, employment history, and even social media activity to create a more comprehensive financial profile. This has helped expand financial inclusion by offering loans to people with limited credit history who might have been overlooked by traditional scoring systems.

Fraud detection has also seen significant advancements with AI. Financial institutions use AI-driven systems to monitor transactions in real time, flagging suspicious activities that could indicate fraud. Unlike rule-based fraud detection, which relies on predefined patterns, AI continuously learns and adapts, identifying new fraud tactics as they emerge. This has led to faster fraud prevention, reducing financial losses and protecting customers from identity theft and unauthorized transactions.

Customer service in finance has been transformed by AI-powered chatbots and virtual assistants. Many banks and financial institutions now use AI-driven bots to assist customers with account inquiries, transaction history, and financial planning. These chatbots provide instant responses, reducing wait times and improving customer satisfaction. Some AI assistants even analyze customer spending patterns and offer personalized budgeting advice, helping users manage their finances more effectively.

Portfolio management is another area where AI is making a major impact. Robo-advisors, which are AI-driven investment platforms, create and manage diversified investment portfolios based on an investor's risk tolerance and financial goals. These automated systems continuously monitor market conditions and rebalance portfolios as needed, ensuring optimal performance. Robo-advisors have made investing more accessible, allowing individuals to build wealth with minimal effort and lower fees compared to traditional financial advisors.

AI is also helping businesses make strategic financial decisions. Companies use AI-driven analytics to forecast revenue, manage cash flow, and optimize expenses. Predictive models analyze market conditions, consumer behavior, and competitor activity, allowing businesses to adjust their financial strategies accordingly. AI-driven scenario analysis helps companies prepare for potential economic downturns or unexpected financial shocks by simulating different business environments and outcomes.

Regulatory compliance is another critical aspect of financial decision-making where AI plays a role. Financial institutions must comply with numerous regulations to prevent money laundering, tax evasion, and other financial crimes. AI-powered compliance tools automatically analyze transactions, detect anomalies, and ensure businesses adhere to legal requirements. These systems reduce the burden on compliance teams, minimizing human errors and ensuring more accurate regulatory reporting.

Cybersecurity in finance has become increasingly reliant on AI. AI-powered security systems detect and respond to cyber threats in real time, preventing data breaches and financial crimes. AI identifies unusual login patterns, suspicious transactions, and potential hacking attempts, blocking unauthorized access before damage occurs. With the growing threat of cyberattacks on financial institutions, AI-driven security measures are essential for safeguarding sensitive financial data.

AI-driven sentiment analysis is also gaining traction in financial decision-making. By analyzing news articles, social media discussions, and market reports, AI can assess investor sentiment and predict market movements. For example, if AI detects a surge in negative sentiment about a particular company, it may indicate potential stock declines, helping investors adjust their strategies accordingly. This real-time analysis gives traders and fund managers a competitive edge by providing deeper insights into market behavior.

The integration of AI in financial decision-making has created opportunities for greater efficiency and accuracy, but it also comes with challenges. One concern is the potential for AI bias in decision-making. If AI models are trained on biased data, they may reinforce existing inequalities in lending, hiring, or investment opportunities. Financial institutions must continuously monitor and refine AI algorithms to ensure fair and unbiased decision-making.

Another challenge is the ethical and regulatory implications of AI-driven finance. With AI making more autonomous financial decisions, questions arise about accountability and transparency. Regulators are working to establish guidelines to ensure that AI-driven financial systems operate fairly and ethically while maintaining human oversight in critical decision-making processes.

Despite these challenges, AI is rapidly shaping the future of financial decision-making. Businesses, banks, and investors who leverage AI-powered insights gain a competitive advantage, making faster and more informed choices. As AI technology continues to advance, financial decision-making will become more data-driven, predictive, and personalized, leading to a more efficient and inclusive financial ecosystem.

Cybersecurity and Data Privacy in Finance

Cybersecurity and data privacy have become critical concerns in the financial sector as businesses, banks, and investment firms increasingly rely on digital platforms to store and manage sensitive financial information. With cyber threats evolving rapidly, protecting financial data from breaches, fraud, and unauthorized access is essential for maintaining trust and stability in the industry. The rise of online banking, digital payments, and fintech solutions has created new opportunities for cybercriminals to exploit vulnerabilities, making it necessary for financial institutions to implement advanced security measures.

One of the biggest threats in finance is cyber fraud, which includes phishing attacks, identity theft, and unauthorized transactions. Cybercriminals use sophisticated techniques to trick individuals into revealing sensitive information, such as login credentials and credit card details. Phishing emails and fake websites designed to look like legitimate banking portals are common tactics used to steal personal and financial data. Once attackers gain access to an account, they can transfer funds, make fraudulent purchases, or even apply for loans in the victim's name. Financial institutions combat this threat by implementing multi-factor authentication, real-time fraud detection, and biometric security measures.

Data breaches pose another major risk to financial organizations. A data breach occurs when hackers infiltrate a company's database to steal sensitive customer information, including Social Security numbers, account details, and transaction histories. Stolen data can be sold on the dark web or used for identity theft and financial fraud. To prevent breaches, financial institutions invest in encryption technologies, firewalls, and secure cloud storage solutions. They also conduct regular security audits to identify vulnerabilities and ensure compliance with data protection regulations.

Ransomware attacks have become an increasing concern for financial organizations. In a ransomware attack, hackers encrypt a company's data and demand payment in cryptocurrency to restore access. If financial institutions fall victim to such an attack, they risk losing critical financial records, disrupting banking services, and damaging their reputation. Many businesses have implemented backup and recovery systems to mitigate the impact of ransomware attacks, ensuring they can restore their systems without paying the ransom.

Regulatory compliance is a crucial aspect of cybersecurity and data privacy in finance. Governments and regulatory bodies have established strict guidelines to protect consumer data and prevent financial crimes. Regulations such as the General Data Protection Regulation (GDPR) in Europe and the California Consumer Privacy Act (CCPA) in the United States require businesses to safeguard personal data and give consumers control over their information. Financial institutions must also comply with anti-money laundering (AML) and Know Your Customer (KYC) regulations to prevent fraud and illegal transactions. Non-compliance with these laws can result in hefty fines, legal consequences, and reputational damage.

The growing use of artificial intelligence and machine learning in finance has introduced both opportunities and challenges in cybersecurity. AI-powered security systems can analyze vast amounts of transaction data in real time, detecting unusual patterns that may indicate fraudulent activity. Machine learning algorithms can improve over time, adapting to new cyber threats and enhancing fraud prevention measures. However, AI-driven cybersecurity also presents risks, as cybercriminals can use AI to develop more sophisticated attacks, such as deepfake scams and AI-generated phishing emails.

Cloud computing has transformed financial services by offering scalable storage solutions and remote accessibility. However, storing financial data in the cloud comes with security risks, including data leaks and unauthorized access. Financial institutions must implement strong encryption protocols, access controls, and monitoring systems to protect cloud-based financial data. Many organizations use hybrid cloud solutions, which combine private and public cloud services to balance security and efficiency.

Mobile banking and digital payment systems have made financial transactions more convenient, but they have also increased exposure to cyber threats. Mobile apps and contactless payment methods are vulnerable to hacking, malware, and man-in-the-middle attacks. To secure mobile financial transactions, banks use tokenization, which replaces sensitive card details with a unique digital identifier, reducing the risk of fraud. Consumers are also encouraged to enable security features such as fingerprint authentication and secure app access to protect their financial data.

One of the emerging trends in financial cybersecurity is the use of blockchain technology. Blockchain provides a decentralized and tamper-resistant way to record transactions, reducing the risk of fraud and unauthorized alterations. Cryptocurrencies and decentralized finance

(DeFi) platforms leverage blockchain security to offer transparent and secure financial transactions. However, despite its security benefits, blockchain technology is not immune to attacks, as hackers have exploited vulnerabilities in smart contracts and cryptocurrency exchanges.

Employee awareness and training play a crucial role in maintaining cybersecurity in financial institutions. Many cyberattacks occur due to human error, such as employees clicking on malicious links or using weak passwords. Financial organizations invest in cybersecurity training programs to educate employees on best practices, such as recognizing phishing attempts, using secure networks, and handling sensitive customer data responsibly.

Cybersecurity in finance is an ongoing challenge that requires constant adaptation to new threats. Financial institutions must remain proactive by investing in advanced security technologies, enforcing regulatory compliance, and promoting cybersecurity awareness among employees and customers. As digital financial services continue to evolve, maintaining strong cybersecurity and data privacy measures will be essential in ensuring a secure and resilient financial ecosystem.

The Rise of Decentralized Finance (DeFi)

Decentralized Finance (DeFi) has transformed the financial landscape by offering an alternative to traditional banking systems. It operates on blockchain technology, removing the need for intermediaries such as banks, brokers, and centralized institutions. This shift allows users to access financial services, including lending, borrowing, trading, and yield farming, without relying on conventional financial entities. By leveraging smart contracts, DeFi platforms automate transactions, ensuring transparency, security, and efficiency in financial operations.

One of the key reasons DeFi has gained popularity is its ability to provide financial services to anyone with an internet connection. Unlike traditional banks that require extensive documentation and credit history checks, DeFi platforms allow users to participate in financial activities without restrictions. This inclusivity is particularly beneficial in regions with limited banking infrastructure, where people often struggle to access loans or investment opportunities. With DeFi, individuals can transact and invest in a decentralized environment, gaining financial independence.

Smart contracts play a vital role in DeFi by facilitating automated transactions. These contracts are self-executing agreements with predefined rules coded into them. Once conditions are met, the contract executes itself without the need for intermediaries. This automation reduces the risk of fraud, minimizes errors, and enhances transaction efficiency. However, since smart contracts operate on blockchain networks, any coding flaws can pose security risks, potentially leading to financial losses if exploited by hackers.

One of the most popular applications of DeFi is decentralized lending and borrowing. Traditional loans involve banks assessing creditworthiness, setting interest rates, and requiring collateral. In contrast, DeFi lending platforms allow users to lend and borrow digital assets through smart contracts. Borrowers provide cryptocurrency as collateral, while lenders earn interest on their deposits. These platforms offer flexible lending options, competitive interest rates, and faster transactions compared to traditional banking systems. However, volatility in cryptocurrency prices can pose challenges, as fluctuations may trigger liquidations if collateral values drop significantly.

Decentralized exchanges (DEXs) have revolutionized cryptocurrency trading by enabling peer-to-peer transactions without intermediaries. Unlike centralized exchanges that require users to deposit funds into a managed account, DEXs allow traders to retain control of their assets at all times. This reduces counterparty risks and enhances security, as there is no single point of failure that hackers can exploit. Popular DEXs such as Uniswap and SushiSwap operate using automated market maker (AMM) protocols, where liquidity providers earn fees by supplying funds to trading pools. Despite the benefits, DEXs can suffer from liquidity shortages and slippage, leading to price inefficiencies in certain market conditions.

Yield farming and liquidity mining have emerged as innovative ways for investors to earn passive income through DeFi. Yield farming involves providing liquidity to DeFi protocols in exchange for rewards, typically in the form of governance tokens. Liquidity mining, on the other hand, incentivizes users to contribute funds to decentralized exchanges or lending pools by distributing tokens as a reward. While these mechanisms offer high returns, they also come with risks such as impermanent loss, smart contract vulnerabilities, and market volatility.

Stablecoins play a crucial role in DeFi by providing a less volatile alternative to traditional cryptocurrencies. Unlike Bitcoin and Ethereum, which experience significant price fluctuations, stablecoins are pegged to fiat currencies like the US dollar. Popular stablecoins such as USDT, USDC, and DAI enable users to engage in DeFi transactions without exposure to extreme price swings. These digital assets facilitate lending, borrowing, and trading on DeFi platforms, offering stability in an otherwise volatile market.

Despite its rapid growth, DeFi faces several challenges that could impact its long-term sustainability. Regulatory uncertainty is a major concern, as governments worldwide are still developing frameworks to govern decentralized financial activities. Some regulators view DeFi as a potential threat to financial stability, leading to discussions about imposing stricter rules on decentralized platforms. Additionally, security remains a pressing issue, with DeFi protocols frequently targeted by hackers. Smart contract vulnerabilities, flash loan attacks, and rug pulls have resulted in significant losses for investors, highlighting the need for stronger security measures.

Scalability is another hurdle that DeFi must overcome to achieve widespread adoption. Many DeFi applications run on the Ethereum network, which has faced congestion issues and high transaction fees due to increased demand. Layer 2 scaling solutions, such as Optimistic Rollups and zk-Rollups, aim to address these challenges by improving transaction speed and reducing costs. Other blockchain networks, such as Binance Smart Chain and Solana, have also emerged as alternatives for DeFi applications, offering lower fees and faster processing times.

As DeFi continues to evolve, innovation in the space is expected to drive further growth. Developers are exploring cross-chain interoperability, allowing assets to move seamlessly between different blockchain networks. This advancement could enhance liquidity, improve efficiency, and expand DeFi's reach to a broader audience. Additionally, the integration of artificial intelligence and decentralized identity verification could enhance security and streamline user experiences.

The rise of DeFi marks a significant shift in the financial industry, challenging traditional banking models and redefining how people access financial services. While it presents exciting opportunities for financial inclusion, investment, and automation, it also comes with risks that require careful consideration. As technology advances and regulatory clarity improves, DeFi has the potential to revolutionize global finance, making financial services more accessible, transparent, and efficient.

Innovation Labs and Corporate Entrepreneurship

Innovation labs and corporate entrepreneurship are reshaping the way businesses approach growth, problem-solving, and market disruption. In an era where industries evolve rapidly, companies need structured environments to experiment with new ideas, technologies, and business models. Innovation labs serve as dedicated spaces where teams can explore emerging trends, develop prototypes, and test new concepts before they are introduced to the broader market. These labs foster creativity and collaboration, bringing together experts from different fields to push the boundaries of traditional business operations.

Corporate entrepreneurship, often referred to as intrapreneurship, enables companies to act like startups while operating within an established organization. Large businesses often struggle with bureaucracy and rigid structures that slow down innovation. By encouraging employees to think and act like entrepreneurs, companies can drive internal change, develop new products, and stay ahead of competitors. Unlike traditional corporate strategies, which focus on stability and incremental growth, corporate entrepreneurship embraces risk-taking, experimentation, and disruptive thinking.

Innovation labs provide a controlled environment where businesses can test new ideas without the constraints of day-to-day operations. These labs often function as independent units within a company, allowing for greater flexibility and speed in decision-making. They work on projects such as developing cutting-edge technology, improving business processes, or exploring new market opportunities. Many organizations partner with startups, universities, and research institutions to bring fresh perspectives and external expertise into their innovation initiatives.

One of the key benefits of innovation labs is their ability to identify emerging trends before they become mainstream. By focusing on future-oriented research, these labs help businesses anticipate changes in consumer behavior, technological advancements, and market demands. This proactive approach allows companies to position themselves as industry leaders rather than reacting to competitors' moves. For instance, financial institutions use innovation labs to explore blockchain technology, artificial intelligence, and digital banking solutions, ensuring they remain competitive in a rapidly changing industry.

Corporate entrepreneurship thrives when businesses create a culture that supports creativity and risk-taking. Employees should feel empowered to propose new ideas, experiment with different approaches, and challenge conventional ways of doing things. Companies that successfully implement corporate entrepreneurship often provide employees with dedicated time and resources to work on innovative projects. Google's famous "20% time" policy, which allows employees to spend a portion of their work hours on passion projects, has led to groundbreaking innovations such as Gmail and Google Maps.

Funding and resource allocation play a crucial role in both innovation labs and corporate entrepreneurship. Unlike traditional business units that operate with clear revenue targets, innovation-focused initiatives often require long-term investment before delivering tangible results. Companies must be willing to allocate capital to experimental projects, even if some of them fail. Failure is an essential part of the innovation process, as it provides valuable insights that contribute to future success. Organizations that foster a culture of learning from failure tend to be more resilient and adaptive.

A structured approach to innovation is necessary to ensure that ideas generated within labs and entrepreneurial initiatives translate into real business impact. Companies use various frameworks such as design thinking, lean startup methodology, and agile development to guide their innovation processes. These methodologies emphasize rapid prototyping, customer feedback, and iterative improvements, reducing the risk of investing in unproven concepts. By incorporating these frameworks, businesses can streamline their innovation efforts and increase the chances of successful implementation.

Collaboration between corporate innovation teams and external stakeholders is another critical factor for success. Companies often establish partnerships with startups, technology firms, and venture capital investors to access new ideas and capabilities. Open innovation models, where businesses actively seek input from external sources, have become increasingly popular. This approach allows organizations to leverage external expertise while focusing on their core competencies. For example, automotive companies collaborate with tech startups to develop autonomous vehicles and electric mobility solutions.

Measuring the success of innovation labs and corporate entrepreneurship initiatives can be challenging. Traditional performance metrics such as revenue growth and profitability may not accurately reflect the value of these programs. Instead, companies use alternative indicators such as the number of new patents filed, prototype development speed, employee engagement levels, and successful product launches. Establishing clear objectives and key performance indicators (KPIs) helps businesses track progress and make informed decisions about their innovation strategies.

The impact of innovation labs and corporate entrepreneurship extends beyond product development. These initiatives contribute to organizational agility, enabling businesses to respond quickly to market changes and customer needs. Companies that prioritize innovation are more likely to attract top talent, as employees are drawn to organizations that value creativity and professional growth. Additionally, fostering an entrepreneurial mindset within a company enhances employee morale and engagement, leading to higher productivity and job satisfaction.

Despite the many benefits, businesses face several challenges when implementing innovation programs. Resistance to change is one of the most common obstacles, as employees and management may be hesitant to adopt new ways of working. Overcoming this requires strong leadership, clear communication, and a commitment to fostering a culture of continuous learning. Another challenge is balancing short-term business goals with long-term innovation efforts. Companies must find a way to integrate innovation into their overall strategy without compromising existing operations.

The future of innovation labs and corporate entrepreneurship looks promising as businesses continue to embrace new technologies and agile methodologies. Emerging trends such as artificial intelligence, blockchain, and sustainability-driven innovations are expected to shape the next wave of corporate experimentation. Organizations that proactively invest in these areas will be better positioned to adapt to industry disruptions and maintain a competitive edge.

As businesses navigate an increasingly complex and fast-paced environment, the role of innovation labs and corporate entrepreneurship will become even more critical. Companies that prioritize experimentation, collaboration, and a forward-thinking mindset will be able to drive meaningful change and secure long-term success in their industries.

Conclusion

A strong financial foundation is essential for any organization to grow, adapt, and succeed in an increasingly complex business landscape. Financial planning, risk management, capital budgeting, and working capital management are critical components that help businesses achieve their goals while maintaining financial stability. As industries continue to evolve with technological advancements and new financial tools, organizations must remain flexible and proactive in their approach to managing finances.

Innovation in financial technologies, including digital currencies, blockchain, and decentralized finance, is reshaping how businesses operate and access capital. While these innovations present new opportunities for growth, they also introduce risks that require careful management. Companies that effectively integrate these advancements while maintaining strong financial discipline will be better positioned to stay ahead in competitive markets.

Risk management plays a key role in ensuring long-term success. Every business faces uncertainties, whether related to market fluctuations, operational challenges, or regulatory changes. Organizations that develop strategies to identify, assess, and mitigate risks can safeguard their financial health and build resilience against economic downturns. Effective financial management allows companies to navigate challenges while capitalizing on opportunities for expansion.

Strategic financial planning enables businesses to allocate resources efficiently and plan for sustainable growth. A well-structured financial plan helps companies anticipate future needs, optimize cash flow, and make informed investment decisions. Organizations that prioritize financial planning can better adapt to economic shifts, invest in innovation, and maintain a strong competitive edge.

As businesses continue to expand into global markets, financial management must also account for cross-border challenges, currency fluctuations, and evolving regulatory requirements. Companies that embrace adaptability, leverage financial technology, and maintain a clear vision for the future will be better equipped to thrive in an unpredictable world.

Long-term business success depends on a commitment to sound financial management, innovation, and strategic decision-making. By maintaining financial discipline, mitigating risks, and embracing new opportunities, organizations can build a solid foundation for growth and resilience. As industries transform and markets fluctuate, businesses that remain proactive and financially agile will continue to succeed in an ever-changing global economy.

www.ingramcontent.com/pod-product-compliance
Lightning Source LLC
Chambersburg PA
CBHW051336200326
41519CB00026B/7439